Endo

Marrying Across Borders is an easy-to-read true story that highlights many of the unique challenges couples face in cross cultural marriages. For anyone contemplating marrying someone from another culture, this book is an essential read. But it will also greatly benefit anyone supporting such a couple – whether in a pastoral role or simply friends and family.

Rev. Trish ffrench

This personal story helps us to identify with those of different race, colour or belief, with whom we find little in common. Misconceptions are barriers to true friendship. Here we are shown a path of discovery with ingredients making for an enduring marriage and loving family. We find 'foreign' customs to appreciate and even enjoy, away from our insular homeland. *Marrying across Borders* is a book for all to enjoy. Read and broaden your horizons.

Dr Godfrey Harverson
FRCR MRCP DTM&H
Former medical missionary, Thailand

Onwards and Upwards Publishers

4 The Old Smithy
London Road
Rockbeare,
EX5 2EA
United Kingdom.
www.onwardsandupwards.org

First edition, published in the United Kingdom by Onwards and Upwards Publishers (2022).

ISBN: 978-1-78815-895-4
Editor: Sheri Newton
Typeface: Sabon LT

Marrying Across Borders

Sheela Burrell

O&U
Onwards & Upwards

Marrying Across Borders

Contents

Marrying Across Borders

Glossary

Aiyah	to express exasperation
Aiyoo	an exclamatory remark
Dosa	savoury pancake made of rice flour and lentils
Ikan bilis	dried anchovies
Kicap manis	fermented dark soy sauce which is savoury and sweet
Kway teow	stir fried, flat rice noodles
Lah	a word used at the end of a sentence for emphasis
Mangosteen	a sweet and juicy fruit with a reddish-brown rind
Mat Salleh	a white man
Nasi lemak	rice cooked in coconut milk with boiled egg, fried anchovies, peanuts and a chilli relish; a popular breakfast dish in Malaysia
Pak choi	Chinese cabbage
Pati	Grandmother
Rambutan	a plum-sized fruit in a red, hairy shell
Rendang	slow-cooked beef / lamb / chicken in coconut gravy
Rotis	flat bread
Sambal	chilli paste
Thirumangalyam	a gold necklace given to a bride by her husband

Introduction

THE WORLD HAS CHANGED IN THE PAST TWENTY-five years. Globalism has made the world smaller. Going abroad for further education, travel and work have made meeting others from a different culture possible.

Marrying Across Borders aims to help internationals who are in cross-cultural marriages as well as couples considering marrying someone from another country. It is also designed to educate and raise awareness about what it means to be an expat in a new and foreign country. This book is my story. But it's not just my story. It is also the story of others like me, men and women who have uprooted themselves from home and country to marry the person they love and move thousands of miles away. I emailed and sent questionnaires to friends and acquaintances in the UK, Malaysia, Australia, India, the US and Europe. I listened to their stories and, with permission, have included snippets of their experiences in this book. When I told an international wife that I was planning to write a book about cross-cultural relationships, she said, "All this time that I have lived in this country, no one has ever asked me how I'm doing."

Every marriage is the union between two cultures, whether or not the two people coming together are from a different country or not. Yet the challenges faced in a cross-cultural marriage are slightly different. Like me, many internationals bring with them the thumbprint of their upbringing – parents' voices still ringing in their ears – of stories past and dearly held beliefs. This book tries to show the complexities I faced as a foreign spouse. It also explores how a new country and culture can throw up uncertainties and doubts. In my early days in the UK, I often felt detached from others, separate and distant. My husband had a life before me. There were friends, relationships and stories that I did not belong to. There was also the history of a country that I was unfamiliar with. There were jokes, comments and local preoccupations that I did not share. So, when my new English friends rolled their eyes and complained about how long the Tories had been in government, it did not resonate with me. When someone joked, "Any country that invaded Poland in the past sixty years shouldn't be allowed to play in the World Cup," I couldn't understand their humour. This book is for all who find themselves the outsider. It is okay not to get jokes; it's okay not to have a favourite football team, to sound different, wear unusual clothes and eat different foods. Most of all, it is okay to laugh, embrace differences and celebrate multiculturalism.

Sometimes the biggest works of God in our lives are mostly hidden. Looking back on the past twenty-five years of living in the UK, I realise how much God has changed me. I have become softer and gentler when trying to understand others and myself. My story has been one of restoration, resilience and change. In these days of turmoil, when issues of race and colour have taken centre stage and threaten to pull us apart, I hope this book will help us to transcend our differences, draw us together and give us hope for the future.

1

First Impressions

WHEN PEOPLE ASK US HOW WE MET, MALCOLM always gives his standard reply, "The *Yellow Pages.*" The reaction is always the same – a slight tilt of the head, eyebrows raised and a nervous laugh.

We long to connect with others, and asking questions like "How did you two meet?" comes from a curiosity to uncover the unlikely circumstances and events that brought two people from different parts of the world together. There is a yearning in our hearts for a good love story which will lift our spirits and help us feel connected. The story of two people from different nationalities falling in love is a story of hope.

When Malcolm was sent out to Kuala Lumpur on a work project, he found himself looking for a church. These were the days before Google, and so he flicked through the *Yellow Pages* to look for a place of worship close to his serviced apartment. One Sunday morning he turned up at All Saints Church.

When our children ask me what I thought of their dad when I first met him, I tell them my version of the story. One warm Sunday morning, the hush of the worshippers who had dragged themselves out of bed for the 8.30 am service was broken by a loud, confident, foreign voice booming, "Good morning, nice to meet you."

Most of us usually sat in contemplative silence before the service started, but not this morning. It was interrupted by a cheerful, deep English accent. I turned around to look at the source of the disturbance. How dare anyone be so jolly at 8:15 am on a Sunday morning! There was a *Mat Salleh* going around, shaking hands enthusiastically with the people on welcome duty at the door. *How can anyone be this excited?*

"Maybe the *Mat Salleh* has lost his way," said my friend Peng who was sitting next to me. *He is such a strange-looking specimen,* I thought. *All legs and arms – and his skin so pale, as if he has not seen sunlight for years.* A couple of months later, a friend introduced us. As I was about to go for breakfast with some friends, I asked Malcolm if he would like to join us. He jumped up rather enthusiastically and said, "Oh yes, that'd be good!"

If Malcolm was surprised, he did not show it, but breakfast was at an outdoor stall next to our church under the cool shade of a large tree. It was not *haute cuisine* but noodles of various sorts and *nasi lemak*, a breakfast dish made of coconut rice with boiled egg, chilli paste and fried anchovies. We joined a couple of other church members who were sitting under the tree, slurping their noodles. A sunburnt Chinese man dressed in an old T-shirt, shorts and flip-flops cooked breakfast from a portable stall on wheels that had a zinc roof, a stove and a large wok that seemed to sizzle constantly. There were noodles, bean sprouts, *pak choi*, roast pork, chicken and sauces on display. "What would you like for breakfast?" I asked, turning to Malcolm. "Would you like to try some pork wonton noodles? They're delicious."

Malcolm looked a little uncertain. "Err... no. I'll have a bottle of Coke, please." He eyed the basic, rustic stall suspiciously and quickly added, "And no ice, please."

I felt a little uncomfortable that Malcolm perhaps thought that our food was dirty and unsafe to eat. Well, I was not going to let some strange white man with pale blue eyes spoil my breakfast. I ordered my roast pork noodle soup and watched as Malcolm inspected us all. If he was disgusted, he didn't say, but I caught a hint of, *Is this food safe?* However, I tried to be gracious, knowing I might react similarly if I were in a new country and taken to a shabby restaurant under a tree which served meals that I had never seen before. But my first impression of Malcolm was, *Man, this boy is too cautious!*

When I asked Malcolm his first impressions of me, he said, "There was a spark about you, but I certainly wasn't sure about having noodles for breakfast under a tree!"

Malcolm went home for Christmas, and I thought that was the end of the story. But Malcolm reappeared again in the new year, as his work project was taking longer than anticipated. He was as enthusiastic as ever, cheerful and bursting with optimism. There was a large singles group in church, and Malcolm joined us for movie nights and meals out. Overcoming my initial reaction, I discovered that Malcolm was funny, witty and a genuinely nice person. He was authentic, without any deep-seated insecurities, and he treated everyone, young or old, as people of worth. This tugged at my heart. As a friend in church said, "How often do you meet such a nice guy?"

Malcolm and I both laughed at the same things and there was the added bonus that Malcolm loved God. He left for a one-week holiday to Perth and came back bearing a stuffed duck-billed platypus as a gift from Australia. It was so ugly that

I tossed it in the back seat of my car with a laugh. Later that week, my mum asked, "Why have you got a giant rat in the car?!"

Even though Malcolm and I were born and raised thousands of miles away from each other, we discovered that there were many similarities that drew us together. We both valued honesty, generosity and kindness. Our faith and belief in God meant that the lines that separated us blurred. We started praying together because we wanted God to be in the centre of our relationship. It was so easy to be carried away by the concept of 'falling in love' but to actually sit down and pray, not just about our relationship but for our family members and wider concerns as well, brought a new dimension to our relationship.

As we got to know one another, we discovered that although we were both Christians, our journey to faith was very different. Whilst Malcolm and his younger sister Anne were dropped off at Sunday school when they were children, I had no church connections. I grew up in a Hindu family and was sent to the temple for religious classes with my two brothers every Sunday afternoon. From a young age we recited, "*Matha, Pitha, Guru, Deivam*," which means, in order of importance, "Mother, Father, Teachers, God." My duty as a good Hindu daughter was to honour and obey my parents.

Despite being brought up as a Hindu, my parents sent me to a Christian school. At school we heard stories about Jesus and sang Christian songs. I was content as a Hindu, and certainly wasn't looking for God. But God came looking for me. Once at a school assembly when I was fourteen, I remember singing 'When I Survey the Wondrous Cross'. Something shifted inside me that day as I realised that this Jesus was different from how I'd imagined God to be. He was not distant or aloof but instead He loved me. I became a Christian.

When my parents found out, my father responded by saying, "Get out of the house and never return home." Too terrified to leave home, I stopped going to church. I snuck out to youth meetings at school, wrapped my Bible in brown paper and hid all the Christian books friends lent me. It wasn't until I was twenty-nine years old that my parents relented and I started attending church. Even then, I was not allowed to talk about my faith to relatives and friends. Once a neighbour stopped my father and said, "I heard your daughter is a Christian. What shame she has brought on your family! That wouldn't have happened in our home. You should beat her with a broomstick and kick her out of the house and never allow her back."

My father recounted this incident to me and said, "Do you know what I said to that? I said as a true Hindu we cannot speak like that. All Hindus believe many ways lead to one God." That day, I caught sight of my father's love for me. Up until then I had believed that the battles were all mine but now I understood the wars my parents had to face too. I had let my parents down and had brought enormous shame to the family name. Now I was going to let them down again.

Malcolm began telling everyone back in England that he had met a girl. After waiting my entire life for a decent man to come along, I now found that I was running away from telling my parents that I was dating a white man. I was petrified. I did not know how my parents would react to me bringing Malcolm home to meet them. I was deeply conscious that I had let them down by becoming a Christian, and now I didn't want them to know I was breaking away from tradition again. However,

Malcolm did not have any such problems. He simply picked up the phone one day and said, "Mum, I've found a girlfriend here."

She replied, "You went all the way to Malaysia to find a girlfriend?"

Malcolm was bemused but did not overthink his mum's question. But then, he never overanalysed what anyone said. I, on the other hand, dissected, scrutinised and unravelled words. What did she really mean? Was there a hint of disappointment?

An American friend at university told me that when her Taiwanese boyfriend came to visit, her parents said, "Home-grown is best." Sadly, parents can sometimes appear modern and open-minded, but when it comes to their own children, prejudice can creep in. Fear of people who are different to us often has a way of controlling our reasoning.

When I told my parents that Malcolm wanted to meet them, my mum said, "Is he the one who gave you that rat?" My parents were not happy. Mum was suspicious of Malcolm. Sometimes it can be the people closest to us who react badly when we break the news that we have fallen in love with a foreigner. Our family and friends naturally want to protect us, but their words can come across as disapproving. My mother asked, "Do you really know him? What type of family does he come from?" My mother, who had been nagging me to find a husband and settle down, now made it clear that Malcolm was the wrong person for me.

There is an innate desire for family members to want to protect us from making a mistake. Fears can abound because the potential spouse is not like our people, he does not speak our language, he does not understand our culture, his ways are different and he is unfamiliar. To them, unfamiliar means not good. My parents also viewed my foreign boyfriend as someone who had come to steal their daughter away from them and take me back to England. "Who is going to bury us when we die? Our bodies will simply be left by the roadside," my dad said.

In Hindu culture, children play a central role in the funeral of their parents. Children perform the last rites at their parents' funerals to ensure the safe passage of their soul to the afterlife. To die without any children by your side is to die as an orphan. It is to die without honour. My older brother had already emigrated to New Zealand, leaving just me and my younger brother to care for my parents. But when my dad said, "Who is going to bury us?" he was not only asking, "Are we going to die alone?" but also a more painful question, "Are you abandoning us in our old age?"

It felt like I had just handed my parents a life sentence. Their lives were so closely intertwined to mine, their hopes were built on my future, their well-being was my responsibility and their happiness hinged on me sticking around. But I was running away. I had betrayed my parents. I found myself fretting about hard choices that were demanded of me. The thing is, Mum had always wanted me to get married. She had tried matchmaking twice; she had sought after temple priests to have my fortune read; she had even advised me, "*Aiyah!* If there are no eligible men in church, just marry a nice Hindu boy. Don't be an old maid."

But the man who could be my potential husband was also a potential threat to my parents' security in their old age. The situation exposed niggling anxieties. My mother sulked for a few weeks, and I realised that the only way forward was to get them to know the person I had chosen to spend the rest of my life with. My mum asked to see a photo of Malcolm's family, and when he turned up with a lovely photo, my mother said, "How come they are all better looking than him? They can't be his family!"

Malcolm had to earn the trust of my parents and they were not going to make it easy. I had to allow my parents the space to get to know him. Slowly, as my parents got to know Malcolm, he stopped being the "*Mat Salleh*" and began to be the person who could talk to my dad about world politics, who enjoyed my mum's spicy fried chicken and who listened to my parents even when he did not understand them. They began to see him as a son and not an outsider.

Despite their initial shock and hesitancy about Malcolm, in time my parents accepted him. For others in cross-cultural relationships, this may be a harder journey. Language and preconceived ideas can create barriers with the in-laws. Every love story has its challenges, but each one also needs to be celebrated and not just endured. We love not because it is easy but because we are willing to be risk-takers, because we have the courage to take hold of what is beautiful and believe in a future where every race is treated equally. Every couple has the power to decide how they want the narrative of their story to unfold and not to allow fear to dictate choice.

I realise that most of the time, relatives and extended family are kind and want to be accepted too. I have been surprised by Malcolm's elderly aunts and uncles who have never known an Asian before, yet welcomed me with open arms. One holiday when we visited Malcolm's elderly aunt and uncle in Wales, they insisted that we stayed for tea. They got out their best china and served us Marks and Spencer's cakes, scones, strawberry jam, sandwiches, ham, sausages and mandarin oranges. Their warmth and generosity was unexpected. When we said goodbye, they thanked us enormously for visiting. Little did they realise how much I was blessed by their welcome. It humbled me. (It has been the same when we return to Malaysia. My Aunt Santhi does not hold back when she invites us for lunch and cooks a whole array of Malaysian dishes.) They all simply embraced us with love. To them, we were family and that was what mattered most. It has made me work harder at not allowing my own nervousness about meeting new family members become a barrier to forming new relationships.

As a mixed-race couple, Malcolm and I realise that our relationship has helped us better engage with people from different countries and ethnicity. At a time when the world is quite divisive about race and colour, cross-cultural marriage can bring a message of healing and love. As for first impressions, Mum, who was initially so apprehensive about Malcolm, just recently said to an uncle, "Malcolm, he's the best son-in-law. He's Number One!"

2

The Wedding

"HOW WOULD YOU LIKE TO VISIT ME IN SEPTEM-ber?" Malcolm asked when it was time for him to return home. I accepted his invitation, and one September evening flew out to the UK. I had never been to England, and I was excited. As the Malaysian Airlines Boeing 747 began its descent, I caught the slight hint of dawn breaking over England. There were miniature houses, cars, trees and long winding roads underneath us. The city of London was waking up. I strained forward in my seat as if I somehow could peer into the intricate lives and stories of the people below me. There is something thrilling about looking at a new country from a plane window as the aircraft approaches landing.

When I stepped off the plane, the cool, crisp autumnal air surprised me. Every country uniquely communicates itself. Landing at Heathrow Airport, my first impression of the UK was that it looked like a place that had aged. It did not have the glistening newness or the youthful exuberance of Malaysia, but there was something enduring about the country. Stepping onto English soil, I also cradled within me the heart-racing possibility that Malcolm would propose.

It is funny, the first things you remember about a country. I noticed the Asian men and women working at the airport. As a relative later said, "When you first arrive at Heathrow, you wonder if you have landed at the wrong one – is this Delhi or Heathrow?"

The man at passport control was white. "What is the purpose of your visit?" he asked me. "I'm here to see my boyfriend," I beamed, relishing the words "my boyfriend". He paused, then looked at me a little concerned and said, "I just want to make sure you know what you're doing."

Did I know then what I was doing? Does anyone embarking on a cross-cultural marriage understand the full complexities and cost of moving abroad for love? If anything, I felt like a tourist on holiday in the UK.

Malcolm's vicar John and his wife Ivy invited me to stay at the vicarage. September is a beautiful time in the UK. The warmth of summer still lingers for most of the day, with glimpses of autumn in the leaves on the trees streaked with gold and amber. Malcolm drove me to different parts of England. We had walks and picnics out in the countryside, which convinced me of the gentle beauty of a place that I had only read about in Dickens and Hardy. It is so easy to be carried away not only by the romantic notion of being married to a foreigner but also by the idea of moving abroad to a different country. Although we were having a lovely time, at the back of my mind I was a little nervous about meeting Malcolm's family. Finally, one Saturday we drove to Kent to visit them. It was a warm autumnal afternoon when we pulled into my future in-laws' immaculate drive. There were hanging baskets outside their front door that actually looked like they belonged there. Nothing in my home matched – not even the front door.

Malcolm's parents were waiting eagerly for us at the door. I was petrified. They smiled warmly and welcomed me. His sister Anne turned up later. She was tall, stylish and elegant. Whilst Anne looked like a graceful swan, I felt like a small, brown sparrow standing next to her. We chatted and I discovered that Malcolm's mother didn't like cats. Now would you believe that? I have a phobia of cats after being chased by a feral cat in Malaysia when I was young. Even now, when I tell people that I was once chased by a cat, they laugh. But Malcolm's mum was not chased by a cat; instead she was the cat-chaser. Whenever she saw a cat in her garden, she ran after it with a water pistol! *Hmm, maybe we will both be kindred spirits after all.*

Malcolm's mother had invited us for lunch, but I could not smell any food in the house. Also, I was puzzled that everyone looked too relaxed. Should they not be stirring something in a pot and watching that nothing boils over? I sniffed the air only to catch the smell of potpourri and furniture polish – not food. Lunch in our home was a mixture of delicious smells of spices, chilli and shrimp paste sizzling in hot oil. We also never sat with the guest just before the meal was served as there would have been frantic stir-frying, chopping, tasting and watching the hot wok like a hawk.

My in-laws' house looked untouched. Everything was in its place, like a show room – no half-read newspaper strewn on the table, no half-drunk cold mug of coffee and no slumped cushions. Here in the home of Malcolm's parents, the cushions all looked plump and coordinated. I was so afraid to even sit on the sofa in case I left any dirt. Then we were called for lunch. Malcolm's mum had got out her best silver and prepared a four-course meal of asparagus soup, poached salmon with shrimp sauce and a sumptuous strawberry gateau followed by chocolate profiteroles. I took one look at the asparagus soup and gulped. It was green and thick like Shrek's swamp. I am sure it must have been delicious, but after the journey to Kent and feeling a little car sick, I could only manage a few mouthfuls. I was so relieved when Anne said, "Mum won't mind if you can't finish the soup. You wouldn't mind, would you, Mum?" Just like Malcolm who could not stomach noodles under a tree, I too had to get past first impressions not just of people but also of food.

"I was in Malaya just after the war," Malcolm's dad said. "I used to play cricket on the green at Selangor Club," he continued.

I wanted to correct my potential father-in-law that it was not Malaya but Malaysia, and that it has not been Malaya since the British left and that was a very long time ago, but decided that this wouldn't be a good tactical move as I was trying to impress them. All through lunch, Malcolm's father studied me, so I was extra careful with my table manners. Anne quickly made me feel at ease with her jokes about Malcolm's previous girlfriends. Then she said, "You are the right person for my brother. You must marry him," and we all laughed. We posed for photos, and I even got a goodbye kiss from Malcolm's mum. I was very touched by everyone's welcome and warmth.

On our way back from his parents', Malcolm said, "That went well. Do you know, when I was young my parents said that if a foreign family moved in next door we would sell up and go!" I wonder if God has a sense of humour. The two people who had wanted to move if a foreign family bought the house next door to them now had to accept a foreign daughter-in-law into their home. If they resented me they did not show it. In fact, they went out of the way to welcome me and make me feel at home. "We hope we will see you again," Malcolm's mum had said with warmth when I left. The word 'foreigner' conjures up all sorts of stereotypes, but the truth is we are more similar and connected than we realise. On the surface our families could not have been more different. Malcolm's dad was a 'meat and two veg' man whilst my dad was a vegetarian who enjoyed his *dosa* and *rotis*. Roast beef was a normal Sunday meal for Malcolm when he was growing up, but my parents, being Hindus, did not touch beef. We ate a lot of rice. The only rice Malcolm's dad ate was rice pudding. We ate with our fingers, the English use knives and forks. We had strong, sweet, milky tea and curry puff for afternoon tea, whilst Malcolm's mum served weak tea, scones and cakes all served daintily on delicate little plates with cups and saucers. But looking deeper, these differences were superficial. Underneath it all, our families were more alike than we thought. Our parents both loved each other, both had been married to each other for over forty years, family was central to both our parents and their values were very similar.

I was coming to the end of my time in England and Malcolm was taking me out for dinner. When the doorbell rang at the vicarage, my host John ran to answer it. "Is that a significant tie?" John teased Malcolm when he stepped into the vicarage, looking particularly smart.

"Maybe," Malcolm replied coyly and smiled. For someone who was usually very confident, he looked a little nervous.

Ivy laughed, "Well, perhaps it'll be a significant evening."

They are pretty nosey over in England, I thought to myself. And I'd thought Malaysians were bad! But perhaps people are the same the world over.

We dined at The Punch Bowl, where diners spoke softly and the gentle sound of clinking glasses was the only noise in the background. The charming proprietor offered us olives, homemade crisps and a glass of pink champagne as we sat to order our food. At the end of the meal, Malcolm became pensive. I waited in eager expectation. If something significant was going to happen, it had to be tonight, or, I decided, this was the last time Malcolm was going to see me. I was not going to wait for him for ever! The setting was perfect, the ambience just right. Malcolm looked nervous. The silence grew.

False alarm. Malcolm paid and we walked to the car park. The air was cool and crisp. We lingered for a bit. *Wait for it,* I thought. *This is it, he is surely going to propose now.* No, instead, Malcolm went over to my side of the car and opened the door for me. We returned to his small bachelor flat that he shared with a friend from church. The flat was a stark maisonette on the first floor. It had a pink bathroom and seventies décor. We chatted, and then before I knew it, Malcolm went down on one knee and proposed. "Will you marry me?" he asked, looking into my eyes.

"Well, let me think about it," I replied. "I don't want to make a decision whilst on holiday. I will give you my reply in a week."

If Malcolm was anxious, he did not show it. In fact, he looked super confident! When he dropped me back at the vicarage, the vicar's wife asked with a mischievous glint in her eyes, "*Was* it a significant evening?" *Gosh, everyone is so nosey over here!* I simply smiled.

A week later, when Malcolm called, I accepted. Everyone was thrilled for us, even my parents. The world around me looked sharper and brighter. I had been single for so long that I had got used to looking up at the stars, thinking, *I wonder if there's someone out there for me?* But now, when I stood alone in my garden and gazed at the stars, I realised how connected Malcolm and I were despite the distance. It was a lovely feeling, knowing that someone was waiting for me on the other side of this planet.

During the next couple of months of wedding planning, we called and wrote to each other frantically. Whilst most couples would have met and planned every minute detail together, Malcolm left me with all the organising for the wedding in Malaysia whilst he planned the blessing service in England. We both had extended families who would not have been able to come if we had the wedding in just one place. We wanted everyone to feel included and so we were going to have two weddings!

The wedding was going to be in April, immediately after Easter. "Hindus don't normally get married in April. It's not an auspicious month," my mum said. "We need to see the temple priest first and fix a date."

"Malcolm and I believe every day is a good day," I tried to convince my parents.

We wanted to honour our parents, but we also wanted to honour God and did not believe in consulting the priest or looking at astrology. My parents reluctantly agreed and were thrilled when later they discovered that the date we had picked randomly was indeed an auspicious day!

I was a lecturer at a higher education college in Kuala Lumpur. Handing in my notice and saying goodbye to my students who were coming to the end of the academic year and flying off to the US to complete their degree was not too difficult. The enormity of my decision as I sold my car and arranged for a wedding didn't really hit me – there was so much to do and organise on my own. Wedding receptions are a big deal in my culture, with sometimes over three hundred guests to cater for. If this was not bad enough, I also had to collect all the evidence for my interview at the British High Commission for a wife's visa. I felt harassed and stressed but, most of all, alone. My Aunt Santhi reassured me, "It's not how you marry; it's how you live your marriage afterwards. That's more important."

But I was also feeling guilty. Although my parents still had my younger brother at home, I felt burdened about their care as they grew older. In my culture, parents are not put in nursing homes in their old age but looked after by their children. My decision to move to England made me feel as if I was choosing Malcolm's family over my own parents.

When I talked to my colleague Miss Chong about my doubts over leaving home, she said, "Your parents have lived their life. This is your life now."

"But does it have to be this hard?" I replied.

"When I fell in love with a guy from the UK, my mum made me choose," Miss Chong said. "My mum said that if I married Ian, then she wouldn't be able to cope. My mum gave me an ultimatum: 'It's either him or me.' You know, I never returned to the UK. Now I tell my mum that I'm an old spinster because of her."

I never really understood the full implication of migrating until I had children of my own. As a friend said, "My colleague in Essex was in floods of tears because her daughter was moving to Kent. Imagine what I must have made my mum go through, leaving my country to settle in England. You just don't think about these things when you're young."

Would I have done things differently? Life is not often neatly ordered and contained. Things happen. Our lives

17

meander to unmapped places; we stumble into unplanned paths and make unexpected choices. An international relationship can alter both our lives and the lives of others close to us.

Deciding which partner should be the one to leave home will never be easy. Either way, one set of parents will lose their child and one partner has to relinquish their career, family, friends and security. Couples embarking on cross-cultural marriages must have a clear idea of where they want to live, where they want to raise their children and which culture would suit both.

Julie, a young Slovakian mum, married to an Englishman, said, "I always feel as if I am giving up something to be able to stay here. My parents are important to me, but so is my husband."

Being in a cross-cultural relationship requires us to talk about 'parent guilt' openly with our partner. If not, continuing, persistent guilt can ruin a relationship. Resentment can grow because one spouse has to sacrifice so much. Keeping options open about where to live in case one location does not fit as home allows for open conversation between a couple. When I met Jill, a Singaporean, she kept talking about wanting to be closer to her family. Even after ten years in England, Jill did not feel at home. Eventually, Jill managed to persuade her husband to move to Australia. Although Australia was still not home, it was only six hours away from Singapore compared to the fourteen hours from the UK. However, when they left England, her mother-in-law complained, "She's stealing my son from me."

There are no perfect solutions and it is impossible to make everyone happy. We chose the UK because it ticked all the boxes. Coming to that conclusion was the easy part. Choices can be messy. Choices can also be painful. However, my cousin said to me, "You are doing all that you can. Some children live just down the road and don't even care for their parents."

My decision to leave my parents demanded faith. Could I trust God to look after them? Perhaps, at some stage, all of us in a cross-cultural marriage face that question. There are things that we can put in place. We can plan for emergencies and keep in contact with neighbours and friends so that they can keep an eye on our elderly parents. I knew I could not do everything for my parents, and I had to learn to surrender difficult decisions to my God, who knows all things and is in all things.

I turned up for my interview at the British High Commission in Kuala Lumpur clutching cards, letters and notes that Malcolm and I had sent to each other. I was asked to wait till I was called to a booth where a very stern-looking English lady sat examining her papers. I reminded myself that Malcolm had told me that his church was praying about the interview.

"Good afternoon," the lady said, hardly moving her lips whilst scrutinising my letters. "How long have you known each other?" she asked without even looking up at me.

"Err, about a year and a bit," I said. Just as I said it, I suddenly realised the somewhat hasty nature of our engagement. What if she thought that I was a fake? The interviewer kept looking down and scribbled intently whilst I sat nervously. The interview lasted about thirty minutes.

A week later, I heard back from the High Commission. I had passed my interview. When I called Malcolm, he said, "Well done!" as if I had passed an exam.

Unfortunately, in a cross-cultural marriage, practicalities like visa application and paperwork are realities that have to be faced on top of all the normal planning. I had to remind myself not to allow the process to consume me. Speaking to others who had been through a similar situation was helpful. We could also read up on immigration rules and be prepared for the visa interview without taking the obstacles put in place as personal. The truth is, it takes more than love to prove that our case is genuine to the authorities. We found that there were a number of legal requirements and forms to fill in. For example, one of the prerequisites for bringing a foreign spouse into the UK is to prove that the husband or wife can support their partner. To do this, they must show that their annual income is at least £18,600 a year.

Unfortunately, our own paperwork journey did not stop on our wedding day. My single-entry wife's visa was only valid for a year. I had to apply for a permanent leave of stay before the year was up so that I would be allowed to stay indefinitely in the UK. Others may have hard decisions to make about whether or not to become nationalised, especially in countries that do not allow dual citizenship. In England, because I am from a Commonwealth country, I have the right to vote, which is such a great privilege and honour. I can still remember how delighted I felt the first time I voted in the general election!

We managed to jump through all the pre-wedding hoops, and suddenly the big day arrived!

Our wedding day was during the monsoon season where almost every day the heavens open and heavy rain pours for most of the afternoon. But the sun shone on the afternoon of our wedding. I wore a red and white saree with gold trimmings. My mum and all the female relatives dazzled in reds, greens, blues and deep crimson shades, whilst on Malcolm's side, they wore muted colours. As Malcolm and I are both Christians, we had a Christian wedding at the church where we met. My family and relatives, who are all not Christians, turned up for the event.

My mum chatted loudly during the whole wedding service to a wealthy aunt she had not seen for ages. As the vicar gave the sermon, my mother's and aunt's voices boomed over the vicar's. I glared at my mum, sending silent telepathic messages to get her to hush, but it didn't work. After the vows and exchange of rings, Malcolm presented me with a *thiruman-galyam*, a gold necklace. This necklace is a gift to the bride from her husband as a sign of love and respect. This was important for my mum, and even though I have little interest in jewellery, I relented to make her happy.

As the heat became intense, the air in the church turned humid and sticky. Malcolm's mother had a funny turn and almost fainted. It rained just as we got into the car for the wedding reception, followed by flashes of lightning streaking across the skies and the rumble of thunder. Our wedding reception was at the Royal Selangor Club, where an array of mouth-watering Malaysian dishes had been prepared for our guests. A waiter snuck in a special plate of roast lamb and potatoes for Malcolm's dad, who did not eat rice. Anne kept saying, "Oh, the ladies here all look so beautiful in their colourful sarees!"

Malcolm gave a glowing speech and said how much he loved me. To hear him say that he loved me in front of so many people felt odd. In all their married life, I have never heard my parents say that they loved each other. I grew up never hearing "I love you" from my parents. Did I feel less loved? Did I think my parents didn't love each other? On the contrary, I always knew my parents loved each other, and they loved their children. They may never have said, "I love you," but they showed it by working hard, by providing for us and by caring. But now, I was breaking away from my culture and embracing a new way of loving. My new culture gave me openness and freedom to verbalise love.

Our blessing and reception in England, however, were slightly different. Firstly, my parents could not join us. I was also surrounded by strangers, all smiling and shaking my hand as if they knew me. I smiled till my face ached. For our wedding meal, we had dried-up roast turkey covered in thick gravy, overcooked vegetables and some bitter, herby balls, which stuck to the roof of my mouth; I later discovered this was called 'stuffing'. Before we drove away from the reception, someone whispered that we had better check under the passenger seat. We looked and found a dirty nappy carefully tucked under my seat! The English have a strange sense of humour. It turned out that two years earlier, Malcolm had left a bag of dung in someone else's bridal car.

Malcolm and I recently celebrated our twenty-sixth wedding anniversary. Looking back, the actual wedding day seems a blur compared to living out our vows and embracing selflessness daily in our marriage. Whilst I can remember some details of the wedding, the overriding emotion was one of joy. My parents looked so proud of me, Malcolm's parents were overjoyed and even Anne couldn't stop smiling. Our wedding celebrations, which centred around Malcolm and me, were also about our parents and our extended families. It was a day of celebration for them as well. My parents, who were convinced that I was going to be single and miserable for the rest of my life, were thrilled to have their only daughter married off. In my culture, having an unmarried daughter is shameful to the family and considered a burden. "Who else would look after you when we die?" my mother used to ask me. Thankfully, this idea that a single woman could never be totally happy or look after herself is slowly changing in my culture. As for Malcolm, his parents were probably thinking, "Oh my goodness! He's finally settled down! We can have grandchildren now!"

3

Moving to England

I ARRIVED IN THE UK WITH TWO LARGE SUITCASES filled with neatly folded clothes, letters, cards, gifts, photos, food, and a mortar and pestle. Three days after our wedding, I had said goodbye to my parents and embarked on a one-way flight to the UK. My dad had carefully wrapped cinnamon sticks, cumin, coriander, dried chillies, *kicap manis*, dried shrimps, *ikan bilis* and a range of spice mixes in clear plastic bags. I think my mother had visions of me starving in England!

"The bag is quite full," I tried to tell my mum. Perhaps this was my parents' way of saying that they loved me, because they could not find the words to articulate their grief. It was an adventure for me. For them, it was a loss. I wish I had been more sensitive to my parents' feelings. Looking back, I am so proud of them for being so brave and letting me go.

On board the Malaysian Airlines, Malcolm had finished his wine after dinner and went straight to sleep.

"You don't mind, do you?" he asked.

"No, of course not."

I was disappointed. I had hoped that Malcolm would have stayed awake a little longer, chatted a little more and paused to reflect on our adventure ahead. But the experience and feelings of the one returning home are starkly different to the one who has left home. For the one returning home, it was a celebration. For the other, the sights and smells of home slowly fading away marked loss. The foreign wife or husband who has travelled far may experience a euphoria that descends quickly to despair because of the trauma of uprooting. Like a plant that needs watering and tending, every partner who relocates needs nurturing when they first arrive in a new country. Just as the newcomer needs to assimilate into the new country, people need educating on how to help someone new to settle into their culture.

Clutching my passport with a red stamp that said "Wife Single Entry", I was no longer a tourist. The officer at immigration with smiling blue eyes said, "Good morning. How are you today?" *My, they are so polite here in England.* Then, the man with those eyes said, "You have to get an X-ray done for TB. Sorry. Did no one tell you? No, I'm afraid your husband is not allowed to accompany you."

I felt betrayed. No one had warned us about the X-ray. Malcolm stood behind a white line and waved sheepishly at me. I felt dirty, unwelcomed and scared. The X-ray department was a tiny, dark room tucked away in the airport with a huge sign outside that said "Health Checks". The others – new immigrants like me in the waiting room – were silent and pensive, heads bowed down. A ferocious-looking lady was in charge. She did not say, "Good morning, darling! Welcome to England." Instead, she looked at me as if I had already made her annoyed by simply being there. She grabbed a dirty gown with smudges on it and, pointing to a cubicle with a flimsy curtain, said, "Take your clothes off and put this on. Someone will be with you shortly to take your X-ray."

I took the gown, stripped and slipped it over me. The white gown with its blotches of brown stain was a stark reminder that I was just another one to be processed. The fact was, just because I had been a resplendent bride three days ago did not make an iota of difference to my status here. I caught the shifty X-ray technician peer through the parting in the flimsy curtain as I undressed. For a split second, I understood the vulnerability of an immigrant in a new land with no rights. *You are a rat,* I thought. X-ray done, I darted out of the room quickly in case I contracted TB.

The sky looked weepy on our long drive to our new home. The clouds had ganged up on the sun, and a greyness clung to the morning like an unwanted visitor. But when the taxi pulled up to our new house, I spotted daffodils cascading from a large jug left outside our front door by one of Malcolm's good friends. A hand stretched out to welcome me, and my spirit lifted.

One of the first things I had to do was to get my British driving licence. This meant retraining someone like me who had accumulated bad habits over the years.

"Why would I need driving lessons?" I asked Malcolm. "Marie is from France. She doesn't need a British driving licence. The French drive on the wrong side anyway."

Malcolm is a practical man. "Well, it's something that needs to be done."

Through Fatima, a Bosnian refugee whom Malcolm knew through church, I found an instructor called Sue who had helped Fatima's daughter-in-law pass her driving test.

"Sue is very good," Fatima said, giving the thumbs up. Fatima had only come to England a few years earlier and so I trusted her judgment on Sue. If Sue could help one foreigner to pass, then she would be great for me too.

Sue was patient. "Did you not see the man crossing the road?" she asked the first time I drove without stopping at a zebra crossing.

"Oh, dear! Is that why he was waving his fist in the air?" I asked. I thought I knew everything about driving but my new country threw up unexpected curves and bends. There were too many roundabouts in England, and the country lanes which Sue insisted on calling "roads" were incredibly narrow. Even a bullock cart would not get through!

My driving test did not turn out as planned. There was just one small incident but it was a big mistake! I was waiting at some traffic lights, but when the lights turned green, the car went backwards instead of forwards. My not-so-friendly examiner turned around and stared at me. I'd failed!

I passed my test the second time around – but there was always more to learn. Malcolm made me aware of bicycle and walking lanes. We do not have bicycle lanes or pedestrian lanes back home. The idea of a footpath was novel to me. "We should not stray into a bicycle lane," Malcolm said. He explained that this wasn't considerate to cyclists. But on our walk to town, I noticed that not many pedestrians followed the rules. I just stared at them, but no one took any notice of me.

Moving abroad in a cross-cultural marriage for one partner means letting go of one life and taking on a new one. Malcolm slotted back into his old life. The Monday morning after our honeymoon, Malcolm strode out of the house purposefully for work. I envied him. I cleaned the kitchen, the living room and then the toilets, but the heaviness in my heart did not shift. I felt alone. Outside our street, not a single soul could be spotted. *What exactly do people in England do hiding indoors?*

As someone from a different country, I wanted to participate, to be involved in British society, but didn't know how. I scoured the local newspaper for jobs and wrote to schools and colleges that had teaching vacancies. Not having any previous work experience in the UK made it difficult to put down references, but our vicar and church members kindly offered to be my referees. However, looking for a job in a foreign country was complicated. My CV and work experience looked unfamiliar. My name was foreign and my qualifications too exotic. After three job applications and no replies, I began to doubt myself. Any sense of significance or value I had in my old country was stripped away. Here in my new country, I felt irrelevant. What was I doing wrong? *Am I not good enough?* It felt as if my qualifications and years of experience as a teacher and lecturer meant nothing in my new country.

Out of a need to connect, I started attending the Tuesday morning women's Bible study at church. At my first meeting, someone asked if they could pray for me – and 'silly me' became tearful. After four months of being in the UK and not a single job offer, I felt raw and disillusioned. The women were compassionate. They listened and prayed for me. One lady in the group said confidently, "You will get a job. Just wait."

Prayers uttered in faith by a bunch of older women who hardly knew me spoke courage into me. I left the Bible study with renewed hope. Moments like these were holy reminders that my God is a God who sees me.

I took long walks into town when Malcolm was at work, and was surprised to see how grubby some parts of the town were. Maybe I had expected England, one of the wealthiest countries in the world, to have clean, sparkling streets.

"But there's litter everywhere," I complained to Malcolm.

"Where exactly did you go?" he asked.

"Oh, only the area near the bus station."

"Well, that's not such a great place."

When Malcolm took me to London, I began seeing England through different eyes. The glossy photographs of Buckingham Palace and the Houses of Parliament only told half the story. Hidden in the underbelly of this country was the grime, poverty and hardship. It's hard to be fully prepared for the idio-syncrasies of our partner's country, for the hidden contrasts and the unexpected surprises a place can throw at us. Things that I had believed about the UK were inaccurate. I was disappointed. Some, like my aunt, who still carried post-colonial hang-ups, thought that white people never dirtied their hands, that they were all rich and smart. So when she first went to Australia, she was shocked to see white people working as street cleaners and rubbish collectors. But a country only reveals itself to you fully when you live in it, not as a tourist but as a local.

Another thing I had to get used to were 'manners'. British people are very polite, and even if you feel annoyed, you will find yourself being courteous. British politeness spills over into everyday life and is quite contagious. In fancy restaurants, where everything is so proper, I sometimes find myself saying please twice, "Please may I have the mixed salad, please?"

There is an unpredictability about British weather which took some getting used to. On glorious sunny days everything looked beautiful, but I soon found out that good weather in the morning did not guarantee good weather in the afternoon. I learnt that the hard way. The wet, damp, cold, drizzly weather that went on for days forced me to stay indoors and stirred a longing for my old home.

The difficulty in getting a job, the aloofness of strangers and the weather made the first few months in the UK isolating and challenging. Marriage, I discovered, did not shield me from loneliness. I still had not managed to even get a job interview. It would have been simpler if God had answered my prayers, but He did not. As an international, it can be frustrating waiting for life to unfold when we already had a life in our old country. The new country can seem like a wilderness – hostile and difficult – but those early months were not without God. I had the absolute certainty of God's hand on my life, and that God had brought me to England. Even in the wilderness I discovered unexpected travellers who journeyed alongside me – like the Tuesday Bible study ladies. Their prayers carried me more than they know. Sometimes the wilderness can be the very place where God chooses to reveal Himself to us.

4

Homesickness

"HOW ARE YOU FEELING?" MY DAD ASKED DURING my weekly call home. "Are you happy in England?"

"Yes," I lied. The truth was, I was miserable. I had only been in England for three months and I missed home. I felt isolated, lonely and far away from everything and everyone I knew. When Malcolm left for work, the stillness of the house oppressed me. Malcolm alone was not enough to give me the anchoring I needed. I was happy in my marriage but I found myself unmoored in the choppy waters of my new life. My new world seemed barren. Without family or friends, I felt dislodged. Were there other foreign wives like me, sitting alone in their kitchens, wondering whom they might be able to speak to that day? Loneliness split my heart into two. At first I did not even tell Malcolm my feelings. Can a tree that stands tall and rooted understand the agony of an uprooted tree? Malcolm is a wonderful husband, but even he couldn't compensate for all I'd lost.

I was homesick. As plain as that. Yet it surprised me. Was I not the intrepid traveller, who dreamt of faraway places, was drawn to distant lands and imagined new terrains? Had my heart not tugged for adventure, to roam freely on this earth, to fly and not be held back? Why was I bawling my eyes out? I found myself subconsciously journeying to and fro in my mind from my old country to my new country. I carried my old home in my heart – large chunks of it. My old country held me, with strong reminders of places and people that made me. The voices of my ancestors, the language and the spirit of the country left behind was alive in me. Sometimes it was the small things like the weather that triggered a longing for home. The harsh winter had been bearable, but strangely it was the warmth of the early spring sunshine that left me with a huge yearning. Feeling the warmth of the sun on my back as I dug the ground and planted deep blue lupins in the garden surprised me with an ache for my old country. The aromatic smell of chilli and garlic when the oil sizzled as I stirred a wok of *ikan bilis sambal* triggered memories of childhood – of being cradled in my grandmother's *sarong* as she told stories and fed me small balls of rice mashed with sardine cutlets and potatoes.

I found myself comparing my new hometown to the city I had left behind. I missed the buzz of Kuala Lumpur with its youth and vibrancy. I missed standing in the packed, pink mini-bus that zigzagged its way through the chaotic traffic, tossing me left and right, my life being held in the hands of a driver who showed no fear. It didn't matter that my city was busy and the traffic crazy, home seemed to brim with life and joy. Chelmsford on the other hand, with its paved high street, was sombre, dull and uninspiring. Nobody smiled here. I missed the happy, smiling faces of strangers in Malaysia. Why was I so emotional? *Stop overreacting. Be brave, be strong. Be a warrior.*

In a cross-cultural marriage, there can be an expectation on the foreign spouse to simply fit into their partner's way of life, culture, circle of friends and family. How do we navigate our way through a world that only belongs to our spouse? I was known as Malcolm's wife and expected to be involved and interested in everything he was interested in – even football! The people all belonged to Malcolm. They were his friends, his family and even his church. Being new in every social circle isolated me at parties, where no one really connected with me. I became ultra-sensitive. I wanted to fit in. It became important that people liked me. But I stood out. I was awkward, shy, quiet and uncertain. I was still the foreigner, and half the time I had no idea what people were talking about. Why did people insist on dropping names of acquaintances with whom I had no association? The effort it took to make new friendships left me weary. People were friendly but often small talk revolved around the same question, "How are you finding our weather?"

After our honeymoon, the in-laws came round weekly when Malcolm was at work to help clear the garden, which was overrun with ivy, untamed weeds and overgrown shrubs. Our back garden looked wild and unloved. My mother-in-law, whom I had taken to calling "Mum", plunged herself amongst the weeds and brambles, pulling out the tangled ivy like a mighty warrior. She seemed to enjoy clearing the garden and took no notice of time or my hunger pangs. We finally stopped for lunch at one. Mum brought out her carrot soup and thin slices of wholemeal bread.

I was still hungry after lunch but had to pretend that I was content. I longed for my own mother's food. Just thinking about it made my mouth water. The realisation hit me that although I had called my mother-in-law "Mum", I could not ask her, "Is there more soup?" or tell her that I missed my mother's food, because we were still strangers learning to love and understand each other. I longed for the easy manner I had at home with friends and family.

Once, Malcolm's mum came to our new home and asked me, "So, what colour tiles will you have in the kitchen?"

The question surprised me. "I don't know," I replied. The question about tiles had assumed that I was already at home in my new country. In truth, I was still struggling to find 'home'. *It is so easy for Malcolm,* I thought. He did not have to do anything, but for me everything had changed. With all sorts of emotions bubbling underneath, resentment grew. Sometimes, I would look at him and think, *you've not had to give up anything.*

People were kind but I felt miserable, and I could not find the words to explain all the various emotions I felt. I felt dislocated, lost and an imposter. Was I the only one in a cross-cultural marriage who felt this way? What if I said to someone, "I'm really unhappy here"? Would they think that my marriage was in trouble? It takes courage to acknowledge sadness and loss. Perhaps we need to give ourselves permission to mourn. Sometimes I wept and wept, but when Malcolm asked me, "Why are you crying?" I said, "I don't know." There were no words in my culture to ask for help when it comes to emotions. How could I ask for help? I wish now I had tried to seek support instead of feeling guilty.

Slowly I did begin to connect with others. When I said yes to the Tuesday Bible study women's invitation to join them, I also gave permission to allow new people into my life. Friendship works both ways. It was difficult to take the first step and join a group that was already established, but once I overcame my initial fears, I began to attend regularly.

After four months in England, I joined Malcolm as a volunteer on a Christian summer camp for eleven- to fourteen-year-olds. On the first day of camp, when sixty-three young boys and girls arrived at the large farmhouse, lugging their suitcases and bags, I felt sick. *Do you know what you're doing?* I asked myself. *You have absolutely nothing in common with these young teens.* There were kisses from mums, awkward hugs from teenaged boys and some tears from the girls. I was in the top floor dorm with eight twelve-year-old girls.

"Hello, I'm Sheela," I said. The girls smiled and chatted with me freely. No one seemed to notice my accent or that I was the only brown person on camp. The main leader and I began praying with the girls and talked about God to them. One day, I drove a couple of girls with another leader to Wales for pony-trekking. We were up on a hillside when we came face to face with a huge truck and I had to reverse downhill quickly. There was silence as the car jerked, then rolled backwards, followed by the smell of burnt rubber. By this time, I was perspiring and praying hard. Eventually, I managed to reverse downhill and allowed the truck to pass. As soon as the truck passed, there was a deafening cheer behind me and the girls said, "Well done, Sheela! We knew you could do it!"

No one had ever cheered my driving skills before. *These children actually like me?* The next day, I went potholing. When I had volunteered, I had assumed we would be walking into caves. As we put on our boiler suits, an older leader said, "Oh, you're very brave. I couldn't do it. I'll just wait outside."

I wonder what all the fuss is about... As we walked into the cave, the expedition leader took us deeper and deeper into the caverns until we came to a gap that was less than a foot high.

"I'm never going through that," I said.

"Yes, you can!" the leader replied.

I watched most of the children slowly get through one by one. There were two girls still standing behind me petrified. I had to lead by example, so I squeezed myself through the smallest gap I have ever attempted to get through and tried to be brave. Then I got well and truly stuck. I had visions of being stuck for ever, unable to move forwards or backwards, decaying in a small cave in Wales. *This is not a dream, this is not a movie, this is real and it's happening to me,* I thought. Then the instructor said, "Turn your body so that you are lying flat on your tummy and then push yourself forward."

I turned my body with my face flat in the mud and damp and thought, *I don't care what I do. I just want to get out of here.* But before that I had to listen carefully to the instructor and trust that he knew what he was doing. I pushed myself forward, kissing dust and mud. Finally, as I pushed and pushed, I saw light streaming through from the other end. One by one we all emerged into the light, leaving our fears behind. Our faces covered in mud and dirt, we smiled and cheered each other because we had achieved something. I was glad when summer camp came to an end, but it made me realise that although I had been a reluctant leader, pushing myself to do something outside my comfort zone forced me to meet new people. Being new to a country, I realised, did not need to stop me from getting involved.

Five months after arriving in England, I finally received a letter inviting me for a job interview for the post of resource leader at a further education college about twenty minutes' drive from home. Two months before, I had been flicking through the *Essex Chronicle* and found the job advertised. I'd applied, but since I hadn't heard anything from them for so long, I had assumed my application had been unsuccessful. Yet here was the letter!

The day before the interview, Malcolm drove me to the college so that I would know the way the following morning. The next morning, I set off, praying hard that I wouldn't get lost, and trying desperately to remember every landmark on the route that I had noted the day before. At the interview, both the principal of the college and the Head of Learning were both warm and friendly and said that they would get back to me soon. The next morning, the Head of Learning called. "We have decided to give the job to someone else. But we were so impressed with you that we are creating a new job for you. How would you like to be the Coordinator of the Learning Centre?" *A new job for me?* I could not believe it! Many times in my life God has surprised me by opening up doors where there were no doors.

On my first day at work, I felt like a child starting school – nervous and apprehensive. Mike, my new boss, met me at reception and took me to the Learning Centre, and then left me to get on with my work. My job was to help sixteen- to eighteen-year-old students who had failed their GCSE English with their reading and writing. At lunchtime, I walked into the cafeteria and sat at the staff table. *Please, please God, I hope one of them will talk to me.* The staff members ignored me. No one said a word to me. Were there rules at work about how colleagues should behave? I had no idea. On my first day, I sat in the large room with nothing to do and did not speak to a single soul.

When I got home, Malcolm asked, "How did it go?"

"I didn't see anyone," I said trying to hide my disappointment. I was thinking back to my old life where I was the academic adviser with students dropping by my office regularly for advice or to simply chat with me. Here, I was invisible.

Two weeks later, just when I thought I was marooned in the large-windowed room, a tutor sent his whole class to me. When I gave the class some work, they laughed at my accent. I cringed at the way I sounded.

"Why, God, have you brought me here?" I asked.

"Do you trust me?" I felt him say.

Later, tutors began referring students to me and some of the lecturers stopped by at my room and chatted to me. Two sixteen-year-olds who could not read or write began to read by the end of two months. A young lady who worked as a cleaner in the evenings and was retaking her English GCSE shared her dreams of becoming a manager one day and owning her own business. The young people were sharing their dreams with me. One seventeen-year-old said, "You're the only one who really listens to me in this place."

I know it wasn't true that no one else cared for these students. I could listen because I had time to help the students who were referred to me. It was my job. It was not always easy, and sometimes I was frustrated because I felt like I wasn't doing what I was qualified for, but God was showing me that even when I couldn't see the way ahead, He could be trusted. He was also showing me that where He wanted me was not always where I thought I should be, but where I was needed most. My young students taught me about resilience and not giving up, and I also learnt that people respond to kindness even if we do not share the same culture. At the end of the year, I was invited to my very first work Christmas social. Having a job gave me a life outside of the home and my initial feelings of homesickness began to shift.

Another thing that helped me in overcoming homesickness was planning ahead for our trip back to Malaysia. Having a date marked in our calendar helped me to know that each new year held the promise of seeing my parents. This was a great comfort for me.

This may not be possible for everyone. Lillian, who moved to the UK from the Philippines, could not afford many trips home, so instead she met up with other women from her country. She said, "Don't just depend on your partner's friendship groups. Seek other people like you who have gone through the same experience but have had a positive experience, not a negative one."

For some, having children anchors us and switches the focus from our own needs to the child's needs. Aunt Santhi, who moved from India to Malaysia to get married, said, "It was only after the birth of my daughter that I began to feel settled and not think about home so much. I had someone else to care for." I found that my children reshaped my perspective on where home is. Slowly, my home became where Malcolm and the girls were.

As I look back and remember those early days where silence was my only companion, I recall how at first I hated it. But then I allowed the silence to teach me, to speak to me. In the pauses, in the solitude of being on my own in those early days, I began to search for something stronger and more constant than my situation. I drew closer to God, felt His presence everywhere – even in my overgrown garden that became an oasis and not a wild, untamed space. Silence can be unnerving, even uncomfortable. But silence can also help us to hear God. Solitude became a gift instead of something to dread.

Although acute homesickness is a very real experience faced by most spouses in an international marriage, it usually does not last. Most of the people who completed my research questionnaire got over their initial feeling of homesickness. As I embraced my new country, I found people who walked alongside me. Belonging to a church community gave me good friends whom I could be real with. Community helped give me a sense of place, identity and belonging. Life began to get better. The pull of my old country weakened, and the feeling of familiarity of my new country grew. I began to look forward to new seasons as much as I looked forward to returning home for the summer holidays. After a while, the boundary lines of home and the new country became blurred, and a new story unfolded with two narratives merging. Home would always be an anchor for me, but for now, this new quirky country with its unusual ways has entered my heart. Perhaps we who are in international marriages are global citizens after all.

5

Identity

"MRS BURRELL, PLEASE," THE DOCTOR'S VOICE PIPED over the intercom.

Nobody moved. A few people in the waiting room looked up. "Mrs Burrell, please come to Room 2," the doctor's voice boomed again.

Whoever this Mrs Burrell was, she sure was taking her time. I looked up to see where Mrs Burrell could be hiding, only to be jolted by the reality that *I* was Mrs Burrell! So, when the doctor called out my name for the third time, "Mrs Sheela Burrell to Room 2, please!" I stood up sheepishly. But as I walked to Room 2, I caught a tiny hint of surprise in the patients' faces in the waiting room. Perhaps there are not many women with sun-scorched skin who own a western name...

At A&E one morning, when I sat with Malcolm's mum, people glared at me. We stood out as an odd pair. My mother-in-law's pale white skin and snowy-coloured hair contrasted sharply with my dark hair and brown skin. Did I look like her carer? Perhaps a helper? But when she said loudly to everyone who chatted to her, "This is my daughter-in-law. Oh, what would I do without her?" people's faces softened. I was one of them.

I was not prepared for the complexities surrounding the question of identity as a result of embarking on a cross-cultural relationship. Being in such a relationship meant holding two contrasting identities that changed depending on where I was. My identity and my status had changed in my old country. I had married a white man, so I was considered rich, privileged and my status improved. For many in the Far East, the white man's identity is still linked to status and wealth, a hangover from colonial rule. In my new country, Malcolm was just another regular guy.

Identities are carved by our families, the songs sung over us, the murmurs of the land underneath our feet, the stories of our forefathers and the people who choose to value us. Before marrying, I had spent thirty years of my life in my native country. I was seen. I had a voice. My voice was not loud, but it was heard. I was known, understood and recognised – as a daughter, a sister, a friend and a teacher. My roots extended many generations, and I carried the name of my family. At work, when I turned up at seven in the morning to grab a parking space in the heaving city, the college security guard greeted me, "Morning, Miss Sheela." He knew my name. When I walked over to the market, where the wrinkly Chinese woman served up freshly cooked rice noodles for breakfast, she said, "Miss, you want same, ah? I pack for you." A nosy neighbour would stop me in the street and ask, "Ah, you're Mrs Muthu's daughter? You look just like your father." At weddings, my cousin and I would be ambushed by buxom aunties dripping in gold who only wanted to ask us about one issue: "So, you girls. Why are you taking your time? Why no husband yet?" Yes, this was annoying, but it also spoke about my identity of belonging and having a place in my community.

All this changed abruptly when I arrived in England as a foreign wife, leaving the people and land I loved for a place that did not recognise me. The first time I walked by myself into town, no one called my name. The wind rustling in the leaves did not sing my name like it did in my old country.

As I navigated my way in England, I found the question of my identity fluctuating between who I was and how I was perceived. *Who am I in the eyes of the people in this new country?* Some days I felt like an exotic foreigner and other days I felt like an immigrant. I wavered from being mysterious to being an outsider, from being interesting to being too different. I hated being awkward, unsure and doubtful. It almost felt like I had slipped on a pair of new shoes with the most ridiculous skinny high heels. Sometimes I tripped, sometimes I hobbled and other times I flew!

As a foreign spouse, my old life had been taken away abruptly and replaced with a new life. I had to start all over again. Stripped of all history, connections and relevance, I had to navigate my way through a country where people only knew me because of Malcolm. Often I felt like a lean-to added on to Malcolm's identity. For the first couple of years of our marriage, my identity was tightly woven into his; I was Malcolm's wife, the immigrant, the foreign bride, the Asian and the 'other'.

Everyone who marries finds that their identity changes, but for those in cross-cultural relationships, especially for those who have moved abroad, the concept of identity can be inextricably linked to the person they are married to because there is no other point of reference for people.

Sometimes foreign-born husbands or wives are not seen or heard as equally as their partners. James from Kenya is married to Jo who is English. He said, "People sometimes tend to overlook me and instead ask my wife for clarification about something which I could have easily answered. They prefer to interact with my wife when it is more appropriate to talk to me." For James this challenged his identity as the man and the head of the family.

We are all guilty of making assumptions about a person when we first meet them. I felt diminished when someone kept their eyes fixed on Malcolm when they spoke, when people forgot to thank me for a gift which was from both of us, when the shop assistant treated me as if I were invisible and when at parties, people only asked Malcolm, "What do you do for a living?" not realising that I had had a career as a lecturer at a private college before moving to England. Suddenly I was just the foreign wife.

Meeting people in Malcolm's friendship groups made differences more pronounced. At parties where people settled into easy, relaxed conversations, I envied the intimacy that they shared with each other. People asked me non-threatening questions like, "How are you finding the cold here?" I wanted the gossip the women were sharing: "Oh, you know Mabel's going out with a new man? I bumped into them at the pub! He looks delicious."

Their conversations were fun, frivolous and naughty, whilst conversations with me were proper, formal and careful. Intimacy was what I longed for in those early days as a foreign partner. It is what connects us more deeply with the other. It is what makes us human.

When I did discover intimacy, it was the most unlikely people who extended their hands of friendship to me. It happened after church at coffee. *Please, God, don't let me be*

standing here in the church hall, sipping coffee all by myself.
Betty, an elderly widow with pink hair, approached me. "Are
you free Tuesday afternoons, my dear? Would you like to come
over for a cup of tea?" I beamed. She was my first friend and
about seventy-seven! "Oh, by the way, do bring your wedding
photos, my dear."

The following week, Elaine, a scuba diver, asked, "Would
you like me to show you the way around, love? I could teach
you swimming as well."

I said yes to both. Betty and Elaine treated me as if I were
an old friend. They were not nervous about me, asking only
polite questions and hiding their vulnerability from me. Betty
and Elaine shared their insecurities with me and their dis-
appointments. There was an easy manner with them which
dared me to reveal my real self. But I was learning a new thing.
In my old country I had been surrounded by friends, family,
academics, students and young people. I have never had a
seventy-seven-year-old as a friend or a forty-something teach
me swimming. I was learning to be open about friendships, to
be generous as others had been generous to me, because it was
in the most unlikely people that I found acceptance and
welcome.

The pace at which I had to learn new things about my new
country overwhelmed me. My first spring in England, my
mother-in-law asked me about new potatoes. She had hovered
over me as I prepared dinner, watching me intently. She was
probably marking me out of ten on whether I was a good wife.
Did I meet her standards? I was so nervous that I thought I
would slice my finger and drop it into the fish pie. Then she
said, "Have you bought any new potatoes? They are simply
gorgeous. Malcolm would love them."

What on earth are new potatoes? Having only eaten old, brown potatoes all my life, I had no idea what new potatoes were, but I could not ask Malcom's mother. So, not wanting to look stupid, I lied, "Oh, yes."

"They taste lovely, don't they?"

"Ah-hah," I replied, feeling so guilty.

It was not just with the family but at social settings too where faint lines of separation appeared. When someone said, "Fork handles," and everyone laughed, I felt adrift. When we returned to my old country, Malcolm got away with not knowing everything because he was seen as a tourist on holiday. However, as someone who had to spend most of my 365 days in England each year, somehow I was expected to know what skirting boards, gooseberries and airing cupboards were, and why the English made jokes about the French! Sometimes they were not even things that mattered. Once, Anne asked me, "Do you have a dryer?"

I said, "Yes."

Then she turned to Malcolm. "Oh, it's good you have a dryer."

"What dryer?" Malcolm asked looking puzzled.

A dryer, it turned out, is not a hairdryer but a machine to dry clothes! How on earth was I to know that? You see, where I come from, we dry our clothes on the line outside where the sun shines all year round.

Unfamiliarity breathed uncertainty. I began to believe that it defined me. It dented my hidden sense of self. I wanted to be at ease with people, but I couldn't keep up with all the new things I had to learn about England. When I told Malcolm about my episodes, he saw the funny side. He laughed when I mispronounced Shropshire and said "Shrop-sharyer", but also assured me that it was okay to get things wrong. Malcolm became my walking encyclopaedia, which was very reassuring for me. In a cross-cultural relationship, having a partner who can explain little things like what is considered polite or impolite in a culture and what different colloquialisms mean can help with confidence and communication. Small things make a big difference; for me, they removed barriers, which helped me relax and be myself without thinking I was going to inadvertently offend someone.

However, the journey to rediscovering my identity amongst new friends sometimes left me with cuts and bruises. Comments from people like, "Oh, your house smells like an Indian takeaway," did not help. A church friend asking, "What do you eat every day? Is it curry?" made me feel defined by other people's preconceived ideas as to what a brown person must eat. (I don't ask a white person, "Do you have roast beef every day?")

At the dentist, the hygienist said, "Your teeth are stained because of all that curry you eat." I wanted to say, "No, I don't eat curry every day. Malaysian food encompasses stews, pickles, fresh salads, charcoal-grilled meat as well as stir fries." But what's the point?

I became guarded because food represented my identity. For some time, I stopped cooking with garlic, I bought scented candles for the house and started spraying our home with perfume. Others make similar adjustments. A friend once said, "Even though my son loves Polish bread, I would not allow him to take it for school lunch, because the other kids will laugh at him. He will stand out for all the wrong reasons."

Sometimes we are so afraid of our culture's beautiful things that we become experts at blending in, because revealing our identity opens us to being vulnerable. So, perhaps in some subconscious way, I have chosen to become less foreign and embrace a new way of dressing and eating to be more like the people of my new country. But the parts of my identity that I wanted to strip away so I would appear less primitive and different have changed over time. There is a shift happening in the UK. It is cool to eat ethnic food now. I have met white people who stink of garlic! It is even cool to pick up your food with your fingers because that is how some foods are eaten. Street food has become trendy.

At a Chinese restaurant in London, a friend picked up her bowl of broth and slurped it! "Where did you learn to do that?" I asked wide-eyed.

"Oh, from my uni mate who's Japanese. She said that's the right way to do it – to get the real flavour of the broth." My mother-in-law would have fainted!

In the early days, I bought myself a Delia Smith cookery book and taught myself shepherd's pie, casseroles and desserts. But I also more recently held a cooking demo over Zoom on Malaysian street food at a church event during lockdown. People celebrated my culture, and other cultures, with me. Being able to cook food from both our cultures allowed me to inhabit two worlds. It has taken me a while, but I have learnt not to be afraid to be who I am, not to allow the narrative of my new country to dictate that the food from my home is inferior.

Once at a party, someone asked me, "So where are you from?"

"I'm from Malaysia," I said.

"But where are you from originally?"

"I'm originally from Malaysia."

"But you don't look like most Malaysians I know. Where were your parents from?"

I was not offended by the question. When people ask me where I am from, I know they are curious, interested and extending friendship. But for others, it can trigger traumatic memories of home. It can also separate people and define them as a foreigner. When I asked a South Korean friend whether she was Japanese, she was offended. My inability to grasp the historical implications between the two countries insulted her. She was born in South Korea but grew up in the US and identified herself as American. Asking people where they are from is not straightforward anymore in our global world. When someone asks me, "But where are you originally from?" it confuses me. My roots and origin are only from the land where I was born in and that is Malaysia.

"Your forefathers must be from India," the man at the party quipped, as if congratulating himself for solving a mystery. His statement niggled at me. It implied because I looked a certain way, then I must be from a certain race. Perhaps people feel the need to define and put boundaries around race. I was itching to ask him, "Where are *you* from originally?"

The struggle I had over my identity during the first few years in a cross-cultural relationship has become less as the years have gone by. Recently, I felt the slight tilt of a change that's happened over time. I no longer feel the need to ask myself, "Who am I really?" Instead, I can say, "I am known and loved in my new country." I have discovered friends of my own, which not only has been liberating but has given me an identity outside of Malcolm. The friends I made were not Malcolm's friends – they were mine, all mine! This helped to heal the disorientation I felt when I first came to England.

I am no longer confused by my place in my family and the church family which is my community. I have a secure anchor within these relationships. Nowadays, I am called Poppy's mum, a teacher or just Sheela. Lately it is Malcolm who has been referred to as Sheela's husband, which I find funny. And things that bothered me before have become inconsequential. I'm no longer insulted when people assume I'll be cooking them curry when it's actually going to be salmon. And when my sister-in-law raves about the ginger and lemon grass in my cooking, I laugh to think I've gone from a curry-cooking immigrant to a food goddess! It no longer matters what people think of me. My identity is something that cannot be stolen by other people's perceptions.

Bits of me from home, like the mortar and pestle that my mum bought for me, the Asian cookbook, a gift from Dad, gold earrings from good friends for my wedding, photos, cards, all kept me connected to the people left behind and to my other true self. It is important to have these reminders in a cross-cultural relationship because it anchors the partner who has left everything when they find themselves buffeted in a foreign land. Malcolm is a good man, and his unwavering patience as I doubted and searched for myself provided a soft place for me, always pragmatic and believing in me.

Finding others from the same culture reminds us of who we are and of our shared story. If you are a foreign spouse, look up international groups from your own country, especially if you are very new to a place. It helps knowing someone else has gone through the same experience as you and has survived! I have also been blessed by people in this country who saw me beyond the colour of my skin, being kind and regarding me as a person of value, and for that I am grateful. But the thing that binds us all, I discovered, was that as human beings, no matter where we are from, whether we are foreigners or natives, we all seek connection, for people we can belong to and to find home.

However, identity goes deeper. For me, it is the awesome certainty that I am known and immensely loved by my Maker. I was known by God even before I was born. God knew my name, He knew the battles I would have to fight, He saw me in all my brokenness and beauty. I do not have to pretend with God. We can run away from who we are, we may be confused, but the constant thread in the narrative of our lives is the heartbeat of God that whispers to us and calls us precious and wonderful. I entered into this cross-cultural marriage full of hope. I know what it feels like to be the outsider, but I have also learnt that my journey, whilst painful, has not been without joy. Every broken bit, everything that has given me joy, everyone who has delighted in me, every day of new discoveries, every scar and every healing have knitted and formed my identity. This is a gift.

6

Food

"AH, I'LL ORDER FISH HEAD CURRY FOR YOU; IT'S very good," our friend James in Malaysia said to Malcolm when he took us out for dinner.

The dish turned up making a grand entrance. The head with eyeballs still intact, softened gills and mouth slightly opened, exposing tiny sharp teeth, sat in a thick, spicy gravy. It looked like a creature from the deep. Malcolm looked hesitant.

"Try some, try some," James said, scooping some spice-infused fish cheeks onto his plate. Now, I know what fish head tastes like. The monstrous-looking head tasted tender, rich and buttery in the mouth. The dish was a delicacy and prepared painstakingly. But Malcolm was not born in Malaysia. Fish was normally filleted, clean and un-fish-looking when served on a plate in England. I observed him quietly. He took a forkful and I waited. "Oh, this is amazing," he said. *Phew! What a relief!* But when Anne, Malcolm's sister, heard that we had fish head curry she recoiled in horror: "What, with the eyes looking at you and all?"

"It's not that bad," Malcolm explained.

"Oh, I couldn't eat that!" For Anne, it simply sounded gross.

Culture and food are interlinked. What is considered a delicacy in one culture is considered crude in another. In some cultures, a refusal to taste what the host offers is a sign of rudeness. When a couple of friends took Malcolm to try durian in Malaysia, he was bemused. Durian is known as the king of fruits in Malaysia. When it is durian season, stalls by the roadside pop up, brimming with this spiky, hard-cased fruit. Buyers squat by the roadside carefully picking up and sniffing out the sweetest durian. Nestled inside the hard shell are pods of soft, rich, custardy fruit which tastes heavenly. But this amazing fruit has an overpowering smell. Some say it is a cross between a drain and a pair of filthy socks. When Malcolm first tried it, he said, "It smells of sewage!"

In a cross-cultural relationship, curiosity and making the effort to try something promote goodwill. Malcolm has never had a piece of durian since that day, but his willingness to give it a go showed consideration and not condescension.

Food links us with our in-laws, friends and the community we belong to. Initially, Malcolm and I were both curious and adventurous in trying each other's food. It was natural and easy. Eating our partner's food when dating is novel and interesting. But eating our partner's food on a regular basis is another story. With the arrival of children, we found ourselves eating and cooking more meals at home. This meant having to choose which type of cuisine to cook. English? Malaysian? A bit of both? Preference for one partner's food can cause resentment. I do not like a lot of bread and Malcolm does not like too much rice, but we have learnt to adapt and respect each other's taste in food (although none of my family will go near the bitter gourds I love, despite my insistency that they're packed with vitamins!) But this can be harder for others.

Sue, who is Polish, is an amazing cook but her husband Simon, a Taiwanese man, refuses to eat her food. Simon was used to food from home; it was the taste that he had grown up with and longed for as an expat in England. Sue said, "I even learnt how to cook Chinese food, but Simon does not like it. He says, it's not the same. So the boys and I don't eat with him any more. When Simon gets back from work, he gets his own dinner. We don't sit and eat together as a family. I never saw this coming when we were dating."

The spirit of adventure gets lost in the surrendering of preferences and desires that marriage sometimes requires. Sue was hurt. "Why can't we eat as a family? It's only food, after all. Why all the fuss?" An unspoken tension lingered. Can two people fall out because of food? The answer is yes.

Things have slightly shifted with their sons growing up. They are discovering a middle ground as a family – food that they can all eat together. Birthday meals have become the plaster in healing their relationship. However, there are days when Simon still gets home at nine in the evening and insists on cooking his own food. Sue has decided that a food fight is simply not worth it.

How one culture values food may vary. In Malaysia our favourite pastime is eating. We love food. For others, such as Sue, it's not such a big deal.

My first church 'Bring and Share' meal was a real eye-opener. Tables arranged in the middle of the church hall held an array of cold quiches, cocktail sausages and cold sausage rolls amongst plates of cold chicken and pasta salads. "Is this what people bring to a church lunch?" I asked Malcolm, a little bewildered.

"Yes, it's only lunch. It's simple and easy," Malcolm whispered, not really getting what I was feeling. I could not understand it. In my old country, the old mammas prepared rice noodles, chicken curry with fat potatoes, curry puffs, spring rolls, steamed rice and beef *rendang* for our church's potluck meals. When my 'judgy' self showed up at these 'Bring and Share' events, I became a curious onlooker and not a member of the family. My assessment failed to take into account the cultural aspect of food between the two countries. In my new country it was okay to eat cold food for lunch, whilst in my old country we ate hot meals. It was what I was used to. I had to move from comparing to understanding.

The first guests to our new home were Malcolm's close friends Mark and Jenny. When I asked Jenny, "Do you eat spicy food?" she said, "Oh, I love a good curry."

I was thrilled to welcome our very first guests. When Mark and Jenny turned up for lunch, Mark said, "Oh, we have been looking forward to this all week." Unfortunately, as lunch progressed, I noticed that Jenny had gone red and was weeping. "Are you okay?" I asked.

"Oh, I'm so sorry, I did not expect it to be so hot," she squeaked softly.

I apologised, then Jenny apologised, and then I apologised, then Jenny apologised again, which just made me feel awful. Later, Jenny clarified, "When I have a takeaway, I normally get a korma."

I learnt that day that when a westerner says, "I love spicy food," it does not mean my level of spice. From then on, I adapted my cooking to make it more palatable to western taste. In a cross-cultural relationship, when it came to entertaining friends, I have learnt to tread carefully. Tastes can be very culturally specific.

Once, when I was cooking dinner, the in-laws turned up. The mustard seed, curry leaves and spices sizzling in hot oil exploded into a smoky aroma that wafted into the living room. At first, I heard a gentle cough, then it was an embarrassed cough, and finally it was an 'I can't contain this anymore' type of cough. *Why do I do this?* Tempering is what we do to release all the essential oils from the spices into the food being cooked – at least that was the plan! Instead, I had released pungent suffocating smoke into the whole house and into the lungs of my in-laws. "We'll just open the windows," my softly spoken father-in-law said.

The next time they came, I cooked pork chops. It is hard to convert people if a specific taste or smell is not part of the culture. Over the years, I have learnt not be offended if people do not like my food or find it smelly and strange. It works both ways. For us who are from countries that do not have a cheese culture, we find Stilton, Camembert and Gorgonzola smelly and disgusting. These cheeses not only look like they are rotting but they make us feel ill. Every culture has unusual and wonderful foods, and being able to laugh at situations and having an appreciation of differences helps.

As a foreign wife in a new country, simple activities like going to the supermarket triggered memories of home. The first time I went to a supermarket, my eyes scanned the shelves for foods that I had been so accustomed to. There was no water spinach, Chinese chives, fish cakes, rambutans, mangosteens or dried fish. It was not a big deal, but it became a big deal to me. I was thousands of miles away from home. I needed something familiar. Food cravings became a new thing for me. I was desperate for a plate of fried *kway teow* – rice noodles with Chinese chives cooked on high heat and slightly charred. I could almost taste the slightly burnt, caramelised edges of the noodles in my mouth. I was bereft. *Where do I find all the ingredients?*

Creativity helps with cravings. One of my students once told me, "As an undergraduate in New York, I couldn't get any egg noodles. I used spaghetti instead. It still tasted good." Very quickly, I too learnt the art of replacing ingredients: tomato puree for tamarind, watercress for water spinach and garden chives for Chinese chives. Of course, these days, ingredients from the Far East are more accessible.

Sharing food goes deeper than just discovering what we do and don't like. It is part of our history, part of us and our families' identity. Stories of how Uncle Frank once ate eight of my mother-in-law's famous profiteroles in one go is repeated every Christmas! Then there is the story of how her can of beef once exploded in the kitchen: bits of scraggy meat stuck on the ceiling and a sixteen-year-old quickly cleaning up the floor, walls and ceiling before her mother got back. Looking at Malcolm's mother, her immaculate fashion sense and elegance, I would never have thought she ate economy beef out of a can!

Food also has a way of connecting us to our ancestors. When I cook for my family, I tell them, "This is what my grandmother used to cook for me when I was little." They 'ooh' and 'aah' at the meal that reminds me of my grandma. This simple dish handed down from one generation to another connects my children to their great-grandmother. My daughters Poppy and Willow ask me to write down recipes from my old country. Writing them down is an act of remembering, of passing down my story to my children. They not only discover food but their roots as well. I want Poppy and Willow to know their heritage. We have our unique family favourites like a bowl of laksa or fusion food that incorporates both our cultures. Perhaps because of being a product of a cross-cultural marriage, food for Poppy and Willow has always been an adventure.

Food is about feeding the other and looking after each other. For me, cooking good food is one way to show my love for my family. It creates conversations, memories and celebrates our two cultures. But eating together is something that we enjoy doing with friends and neighbours as well. Someone once said to me, "You have a gift for hospitality." She made it sound as if it were easy. The truth is, cooking for others can be exhausting but sharing a meal with friends brings joy. It sucks out our differences, our awkwardness and creates warmth. We forget about the colour of our skin, our age and even our funny accents. A friend said that when her vicar who had dropped by unannounced joined them for dinner, it made her feel accepted even though she was from another country. When we eat together, we relax and welcome friendship. An invitation to eat becomes an open door to share our lives with each other.

The first miracle Jesus performed was at a wedding where people were feasting and drinking. Perhaps, when we cook and welcome others, miracles happen. There is a deepening of friendship and an open invitation that says, "Come and walk with me. Do not be alone."

7

Racism

"THEY'RE ALL RACIST IN ENGLAND," A FRIEND warned me before the wedding. "You wouldn't survive there." I longed for a different narrative to that of my friend who had spent four years studying Law in England.

When I first arrived, Malcolm's family, church members and neighbours welcomed me with openness and warmth. Our next-door neighbour Dave spoke to me kindly and said, "You're so brave to leave home." He brought my bins in for me on bin days, and always stopped and chatted whenever he saw me.

One of the mums in the street stopped and said, "Oh, you've come such a long way to marry. It's so romantic." She sounded thrilled for me and excited. The neighbour opposite us invited me for coffee and we sat and talked about Jane Eyre and Austen. When the evenings got dark and I felt the iciness of my first winter in England, Janet, who lives down the road, baked a cake for me and said, "I'll be your mum in England. There's always room for one more in my life." When my youngest daughter was too ill to make the walk to school with her big sister and me, my elderly neighbour Daphne sat with her and read Brown Bear stories until I got home.

Whilst they were all generous and kind, I knew the cocoon I lived in would not necessarily prepare me for a different biosphere of people whom I had yet to meet, people who were not curious about me, to whom I mattered very little. However, I was hopeful – defiant even. Racism only happened to others; it happened to people who could not speak English, to people who dressed differently, who looked like 'freshies', not to me. So, when I sat alone in the Learning Centre in the early days of my first job, I wondered why a co-worker dropped in weekly to interrogate me. His curiosity about what I did the whole day was full of hostility. One dark winter evening, he poked his head into my office and said, "I see you've got a landline in your office. How convenient! So easy for you to call your country now." He did not laugh when he said this. The thing with racism is that words spoken so casually can wound without leaving any evidence. His open hostility surprised me. I felt bullied, ruffled and confused. What did he actually mean?

When a bunch of boys at a footpath shouted, "Oi, Paki! Go home!" their immaturity was intimidating but not personal. But when a white colleague at work spotted my husband from afar and blurted out, "What a shame he married you. He's so tall as well. He would have been perfect for Laura," I felt rejected.

I vividly remember my first postnatal class where the health visitor asked us to pair up with the person next to us. The mums on either side of me turned and moved away quickly, while I just stood alone in the middle of the circle with no partner and wondered why it hurt so much.

Covert racism is hard to detect. It can be a subtle look, an act of dismissing the other, a simple body gesture or casual micro-aggression. Being married to Malcolm did not shield me from racism. As a person in a cross-cultural relationship, I sometimes face it even now, but Malcolm is often totally unaware that it is even happening. Being in a cross-cultural relationship does not mean that our association with our partner's culture makes us one of them. Our nearness to Englishness does not necessarily mean that we will be accepted.

Of all people, I would have thought that Sonya would have fitted in perfectly with the school mums. White, blonde and married to an Englishman, Sonya was sophisticated as well. "I've tried so hard, but it's no use. The minute I open my mouth and the mums find out that I'm Eastern European, they are not interested in me," she confided in me one day.

Sonya felt alienated at the school playground and ignored. Yes, there are cliques in the school playground, but it is a lot harder if the parent is from another culture, even if their partner is English. Playground racism faced by mums who are foreign-born is real, and comes as a shock as it is the last place you expect to find it. Do not take this personally. I have had mums in my children's class who have never once acknowledged my presence or smiled at me. The thing is, seven years of primary school will pass. Do not be anxious about whether your children will make friends. Kids are resilient and the chances are that they will make friends easier than you. I did find some good friends in the school playground eventually. Although they were all English, I sensed that in many ways, they were rebels who did not fit the norm and or they were well travelled and enjoyed meeting people from other cultures. So, if you are a mum or dad in a cross-cultural marriage and find it difficult to fit in at the school gate, take heart, it will get better and you will make some good friends.

In a cross-cultural relationship, there will be instances where unintentional comments can come across as being racist.

A joke in one culture will be racist in another. There needs to be cultural sensitivity and respect, instead of, "Oh, why don't you just chill? We're just having a laugh." As internationals, casual micro-aggressions that go unnoticed by the rest of the world are noticed by us. Perhaps we are too sensitive, but racism devalues people.

Covert racism has a way of burrowing deep inside our insecurities, making us guarded and doubting others. So, when we walked into a cosy countryside pub with friends who were visiting from Malaysia, I became acutely aware of how out of place we must have looked – four brown people and one white man. I felt uncomfortable, unsettled and anxious, because deep in my psyche I felt pubs were only for white people. Of course, nothing happened. Instances like these prise open my own prejudices, where I think the worst of others – it is very easy for us all to believe in stereotypes.

The challenge for me as an international is knowing how to live without constantly mistrusting others. I asked a friend from Nigeria whether she has faced a lot of racism in the UK. She said, "I choose not to analyse if someone is being racist or not. To overthink can sometimes create distance rather than draw us closer."

We could easily be battered and bruised if we allowed the voices of those who inflict pain to become louder than the voices of those who offer grace. And there were, thankfully, many positive voices. Just like the man who poked his head into my office, my manager Mike also poked his head in, but he said, "There's no room for racism in this college. We are here to support you." The women at work gathered around me when they heard about the subtle racism towards me. My sixteen-year-old students at the college hugged me and said,

"Err, miss, we're gonna miss you so much," when I told them that I was leaving for another job. All these individuals and groups of people are white and never treated me as less than them. In fact, they treated me as someone dearly loved. Light shines even in dark places.

To talk about racism as a trait belonging to one group of people would be unfair and inaccurate. At an Indian restaurant where Malcolm and I met up with some friends for our annual pre-Christmas buffet lunch, an Indian waiter asked me, "Why did you marry one of them? Why did you not marry our people?" The question was asked under the veil of a gentle smile. No one in my group knew what the waiter had whispered to me, unheard by the others with me. For some reason, I felt both humiliated and angry, protective of my white friends and sad for this young man who saw the world as 'them' and 'us'. If we are going to discuss racism in cross-cultural marriages, then we must move beyond the premise that only white people are racist and seek to see with clarity that racism exists in every culture. The question, "Why did you marry one of them?" sent out a loud message about 'us' and 'them'. I was judged for marrying a white man. The question made me uncomfortable. In some cultures, white people are seen as having loose morals and being drunks, a stereotype that extends to both men and women. Sometimes our lack of understanding of other races can make us fear the other. Why are we all fighting with each other? Perhaps we who belong to two cultures are uniquely placed to be able to offer understanding. Only when voices of grace speak louder than voices of mistrust can we even begin to move forward.

There is racism embedded within each culture. In my country, being lighter is a symbol of higher class and a darker skinned person is less valued. The idea of pale skin in many eastern cultures as being more beautiful than dark skin has little to do with westernised ideas and more to do with status and wealth. This idea is a legacy from ancient times, where pale skin symbolised the privilege of the wealthy who did not have to work in the fields under the sun. When I was a little girl, my grandma would tell me off for playing outside: "Don't play too long in the sun. You will get dark. Then no one will marry you."

As an Asian woman dating a white man, there were times when I felt judged by my own people. Surprisingly, it is the men from my culture who seemed offended. Was I just a casual distraction for a western expat working in the Far East or was this an authentic relationship? Dating a white man in an Asian culture can sometimes feel demeaning. I noticed the judgemental looks and gestures that said, "You think you're better than us?" whilst Malcolm was blissfully unaware of them.

A Japanese friend who was dating an American said, "I get looks from the local men here when I'm out with Gary as if I'm just a social escort." When a Chinese friend from university married an African American, some of the girls laughed, "Ha, ha! Her kids will be black!" You see, even amongst those in Far Eastern cultures, marrying a white person is marrying up and marrying a black person is marrying down. When my daughter was born, one of the first questions my relatives in Malaysia asked was, "Is she fair or dark?" Mixed white children in my country are deemed more attractive and unique than a local child. Who told us how to label beauty?

Because the concept of beauty is so relative, being in a cross-cultural relationship can make us question our own idea of beauty and fashion. Little comments like, "Oh, that's a bright top!" or, "That's a very Indian-looking top," have made me cringe. I didn't want my 'foreignness' to stand out, because I felt it sent out the message that I was unsophisticated. Standing out meant vulnerability and a target for racist comments I did not want to deal with. But God is constantly challenging me, pushing me beyond the fears and walls I have built around myself. I am learning each day to embrace my ethnicity, to be the person God has created me to be. At my daughter's graduation, I applauded the African mothers who had turned up in their African gear complete with head wrap and brightly coloured dresses. Wow! What a celebration of their culture. For too long, I had allowed the comical accent of foreigners depicted on TV and the stereotypes of my race to shame me. My journey has led me to a place where I can celebrate the authenticity of my ethnicity.

Sometimes racism can be a lot closer. When my youngest daughter was born, my mother-in-law took one look at her and proclaimed, "She looks like your people!" Strangely, instead of being angry, I found it funny. *What does "your people" even mean?* My grandmother used to tell us, "No matter what colour we are, brown, white or black, when a knife goes under our skin, all our blood is red. Underneath, we are all the same after all."

You see, sometimes what is unfamiliar scares us. May, who is Chinese, was upset when her friend, a white grandma with a Chinese daughter-in-law, said, "Oh, I do hope my grandchildren don't look Chinese." I wonder if she loved her grandchild less because the child looked Chinese? My own mother-in-law was devoted to her grandchildren and loved them dearly, despite declaring that one of them looked like "your people". In fact, I think secretly Grandma was very proud of her grandchildren and their mixed ethnicity, and enjoyed showing them off to her friends.

My children, Poppy and Willow, belong to two races but have a loyalty to one country – the country that they were born in. They will always be people of two cultures with a worldview that crosses over oceans and boundaries. Their peers accept them, and being born in the UK, there is a shared narrative with their friends. That makes them more similar than different. I'm thankful that they have not faced racism. Race is not an issue for them although people are curious and ask, "Are you Spanish? Maybe Arabic?" Poppy and Willow laugh. They think it is funny how people feel the need to define them. They are, however, more aware of race and how people are treated because of their ethnicity. Perhaps having a parent who is from another country has educated them on the subtleties of ethnicity and race.

Racism is a difficult and complex issue that will always be there for us who are in a cross-cultural relationship. It arouses anger, hurt, injustice, fear and sometimes laughter. I still find myself muttering "Karens!" under my breath when a bunch of white women take up the whole pavement and I am forced to walk in the road. *Why don't those women move out of the way?* But even as I think this, I feel challenged. *How many times have people moved aside for me to let me pass and even smiled at me? Numerous times. I long for the day when I will change.*

Recently, I met up with two ex-colleagues for lunch. They are both white. We were so excited because it had been over a year since we last saw each other face to face due to lockdown. As we chatted and talked about national issues, one of them said, "We don't see you as being any different because of your skin colour. To us, you are one of us."

When my parents visited us one year, they found the people in England polite and respectful. "People say good morning to us at the bus stop," my dad said, quite surprised. Most of the people my parents met were retired pensioners on the bus who had the time to stop and chat. The elderly people are indeed welcoming and kind, a trait noticed by some of the international students I worked with at the university. One student told me that her elderly landlady made cakes and biscuits for her, so she in return cooked Chinese food for her. But it is not just the elderly who are friendly. Sophia, who is Italian, said, "We left Italy because my husband, who is African, faced racism there. The UK is a much more tolerant country."

As a couple, both Malcolm and I are aware of the extremes of both our cultures as well as their gentleness. We sadly hear of friends being told, "Go back where you came from," as well as the many more positive stories. Sadly, people fear the 'other' when they have been taught that the foreigner has come to steal their jobs, their men and even their children's places at grammar schools. Just as I yearn for those in my new country to get to know me before judging me, I know I too must make an effort not to shut people out. Joining a book club, being part of a church and getting a job forced me to meet people whom I would have ordinarily thought of as unfriendly.

We truly belong to each other when we share our lives with one another. There are so many people, like my colleagues, who point to a grander narrative of how God looks at each of us – equal, loved and included. There are good people around. It is hard to be in the minority, but with time I am learning to remove the layers of fear and suspicion that I have allowed to build up because of past experiences. To have open hands and an open heart makes me vulnerable, but it also allows me to see deeply into the soul of another, to be authentic, to break down fences and barbed wire. We live with choices each day and so I choose to acknowledge the other, to stop and chat to a stranger, to discover true community. The worst that can happen is rejection, but the best that can happen is worth the risk taken. As someone from another culture, I know that past hurts can sometimes still sting. Only if we are willing to move on from the past, to talk openly about our woundedness and forgive those who have hurt us, can real restoration happen.

8

Social and Cultural Norms

"WHEN CAN I MEET YOUR PARENTS?" MALCOLM asked after we had only been dating for a few months. I thought he was joking. Why the urgency, I wondered, when he seemed vague about making a commitment?

Also, the concept of wanting to meet my parents made me wonder if he was serious or simply curious. I was confused by the western concept of 'dating around' to find the right person. The idea of 'dating around' without commitment is frowned upon in my culture.

"But how will you get to know a person if you don't go out with them?" Malcolm asked.

"Well, if you want to get to know someone, you go out in a group. The concept of dating around till you have found the right person is simply not done here. You only date if you are seriously thinking marriage."

When two people from different cultures fall in love, they come as two uniquely wrapped packages with intricate layers of beliefs and rules from their own culture. These beliefs and rules are only confronted when the beautifully wrapped layers are removed and the different ideas about life, parents and expectations of culture surface. Malcolm and I had both lived abroad, yet when it came to understanding the rules and sensitivities of each other's culture, it demanded insight and a new way of learning. Every culture has a different way of looking at life, dealing with conflict and understanding relationships and gender roles. We realised that we needed to respect and compromise as a couple in a cross-cultural relationship when it came to each other's culture.

Our differences became apparent very early on when we began dating. In a lot of eastern cultures, dating is exclusive and leads to marriage. In the West, dating is more casual, with little commitment, and does not necessarily lead to marriage. Although Malcolm and I share the same faith, we did not share a common culture. Some things had to be worked through.

I was uncomfortable about introducing Malcolm to my parents, because he was of the wrong race and there was no clear indication of our status. Was he a casual boyfriend, potential husband or a just a good friend? How would I introduce him? The social norms of both our cultures meant that our perspectives on dating did not match. There was also the concept of 'saving face' in in my culture. It would shame my parents if I brought a boyfriend home and it did not lead to marriage.

Malcolm did not understand the many layers of relationships in my culture, the constant prying and probing by my community. If Malcolm was spotted anywhere near me, the Asian F.B.I. would summon my mum for some serious interrogation about the white man lurking in our house. If Malcolm met my relatives, my aunties would cross-examine my mum, "When's the wedding?" Little things like this bothered me but Malcolm was unaware of them. Malcolm grew up in an environment where there was no need to hide, to keep secrets, to hold things close to the heart. So he could not understand why he had to be smuggled in each time he came to see my parents. I was grateful that although Malcolm could not understand some of the rules of my culture, he still accepted them. One night, when Malcolm drove me home, I spotted my aunts and cousins outside my parents' home just as we were about to pull in. So we drove round the block twice, parked at the end of the street and waited in the dark like giggling teenagers until my aunt and the rest of the troupe left.

As a new spouse in England, I had to get used to how friends are not expected to turn up unannounced at someone's house. In my old country relatives and neighbours would pop round unannounced at any time of the day. In fact, when I was young, the front door was usually left open. Grandma would only shut the door when the midday heat crept into the house like an uninvited guest signalling the time for an afternoon nap. Our home felt busy and joyful as a child, with guests sometimes dropping by at eight in the evening and staying till ten. But here in my new country there is a distance, a separation, an unspoken understanding that shouts privacy. Turning up unannounced is not something people are used to in England. They may not invite you in and simply chat with you at the door. Do not take this as a sign of unfriendliness. Having said that, sometimes I have had friends invite us in when we have turned up unannounced on the doorstep. My friends back home still tease me, "Don't be like the British. I hope, when I visit you, I won't have to make an appointment to see you."

In Malaysia hospitality always centres on food. Here in England when someone says, "Come round for a drink," they really do mean come over for a drink. This caused a small problem with us. When Malcolm suggested, "Let's have some people round for drinks and nibbles," I rolled my eyes at him.

"What! And not feed them?" It did not feel generous or hospitable. It has taken me a long time to get used to the idea of peanuts and wine. My family always offered food when unexpected guests arrived. Somehow, Grandmother managed to serve up a feast from her bottomless clay pot of coconut curries and vegetables to feed our guests. If not, there would always be an omelette. Once, a shoeless beggar turned up at our door at midday. In his tattered shorts and long white beard, the man asked Grandmother for some water and whatever food she had. She quickly went into the kitchen and scooped up some rice, fish and vegetables, and served him. "Never turn away someone hungry," she said to me. How she managed to feed so many people is still a mystery to me.

Once, when Malcolm and I were in Malaysia, we visited my aunt. My cousin quickly went into the kitchen and brought out a feast, despite us having told them that we had only just had lunch. So as not to insult them, we ate what we could. We always put on weight after a holiday in Malaysia! Poppy and Willow associate Malaysia with food and hospitality. One summer holiday after our trip there, we returned home and the quietness of our ordered life in England was noticeable. Poppy remarked, "It's so quiet here in England. It feels lonely."

Cultural differences can create misunderstandings because of expectations. When my friend Maria asked her husband why he never bought her flowers, he said, "Why do you want flowers? They are only for the dead in my country."

I know Maria is dearly loved, but I hope one day she will be surprised with a bunch of flowers. However, sometimes cultural differences can go deeper. When it comes to gender roles, sometimes men and women have different expectations. I grew up in a household where my mum did everything in the house from the cooking to the cleaning. This did not mean my dad did not love my mum. After we were married, I was surprised when Malcolm sometimes cooked, made me a cup of tea and helped in the house. The act of serving the other, without complaining, without even asking, spoke loudly about loving the other. I realised that coming from another culture does not need to define our behaviour or how we treat others. Love breaks inequality.

The way that the English operate can sometimes be puzzling and can only be understood by living in the UK, observing others, making mistakes and not being afraid to socialise. It can be hard, but retreating and hiding will only make things worse. The English are very polite. The trouble is their politeness can sometimes come across as not being open and instead being somewhat reserved. As internationals married and living in England, we carry with us a persistent nagging doubt of having offended someone unintentionally by what we have said.

The truth is, it takes a long time to get to know people. Most English people tend to hide their true thoughts out of politeness. When an English person says, "It's fine," we feel uneasy since we sense it's probably not fine at all. As internationals, what are we expected to do when someone just smiles and says everything is okay? The statement, "It's fine," is vague and unsettling for us from another culture. Once, I asked a guest if they found the food too spicy. They politely replied, "It's fine. Just a tad spicy," whilst coughing and spluttering. In my culture, if someone came round for dinner and I almost choked them by putting too much chilli in the food, they would say, "*Aiyoo!* Why so hot, ah?"

It takes time to grow in confidence and understanding of people's mannerisms in our new country. But the journey can be fun as well as a learning curve.

Talking to other foreign spouses, I discovered some things about British culture that we feel similar about. We simply cannot relate to the enthusiasm the British have for quiz nights. As a Slovakian friend said, "For the English, it's entertainment, but I just don't get it. I don't find it enjoyable at all."

I find quiz nights tedious. Firstly, most of the questions are based on British society and culture. Secondly, quiz nights go on for too long and people take it far too seriously. It also brings out the competitive streak in some. I keep trying to run away from quiz nights, but they follow me everywhere. There's the school's P.T.A. quiz night, a seventieth birthday quiz night, a fundraising quiz night for a teenager's trip to Zimbabwe and finally a church Zoom quiz night during lockdown. *Why don't they simply do a meal? Do these people not enjoy cooking?*

Then, of course, there are the regulars who go to all the quizzes, who win all the quizzes they go to and love answering obscure questions like, "Which bird does the largest poo on earth?" One year we took my mother-in-law, who was in the early stages of dementia, to a church quiz. She sat through the whole evening smiling and then perked up when the Quiz Master asked, "Which ladies' garment did they use for parachutes in World War Two?"

My mother-in-law leaned into the group and whispered, "Ladies' stockings!" It was the right answer! Everyone said, "Well done!" and my mother-in-law beamed. If you are an international spouse and do not enjoy quiz nights, give it a go. Who knows, unlike me, you may get to like them! They may give you an opportunity to meet new people.

Another characteristic about British life that I did not fully appreciate was the idea of going to a pub just for drinks. On arrival at a pub, I discovered that some people in our group had already had dinner at home! Turns out, they only came out for a pint. And then it got even stranger. Those who wanted to eat ordered ham, eggs and chips or a shepherd's pie! Why would anyone take the trouble to come out on a cold, dark evening just to eat something that could be cooked at home? Of course, it took me years to finally understand that a pub with its casual and homely atmosphere helps people relax, chat and connect with others. Pubs also build community.

However, there is another side to drinking in this country that some internationals do not understand: binge-drinking. When I was working as a student adviser at a local university, one of my international students complained, "Why do the English students do this? Friday night is the worst. They get so drunk, they do silly things. I saw one student fall into a bin. He looked so stupid as well, but the worst thing is we can't sleep because they make a lot of noise!" *Why do I feel a strong sense of loyalty towards the English students?* I tried to explain that they are not bad people. For us from another culture, seeing intoxicated young men and women swaggering down the high street is both novel and uncomfortable. There will be things in our new country that we would feel uneasy about, but that does not mean we stop finding what connects us rather than what divides us.

The Brits tend to moan about the weather a lot. They moan if it is too cold and they also moan when it is too hot. When I bumped into Old Tony one day, he said, "Oh, it never stops raining." When I saw Old Tony again the following week, he said, "It's raining again," as if I couldn't tell! But talking about the weather made us both pause for a moment of friendship. Grotty or good weather triggers conversations with strangers. I can be standing behind a little old lady in a queue in the Co-op and we can say to each other, "Oh dear! When is this rain going to stop?" I discovered that this is normal.

The weather also does something to the British psyche. Winter subdues people, but when the temperature soars, there is almost an unleashing of wildness in the spirit of the British. Speeding cars, shirtless men, loud gaggles of young people hanging outside pubs signify the arrival of summer. There is also the hint of optimism in the air – people smile more, young couples lie on the grass soaking up the sun, and gardens are transformed. I realised that the Brits talk about the weather so much because it is very unpredictable. Coming from a country where the temperature usually stays the same all year through, the weather is not something we notice except when it is too hot. We also tend to stay away from the sun. After all, we get it 365 days a year.

The first funeral I attended in England was my father-in-law's. He was much-loved and a dear soul, but there was no chest-beating or wailing at the wake like there would have been in Malaysia. I was also told that our daughter who was two years old could not attend her granddad's funeral! This was his only grandchild, so I was a bit disappointed about this decision. I found the English hid their feelings.

When my grandfather died, all the aunts, uncles, cousins and the whole street turned up. Mourning was not meant to be done alone. The community rose to comfort and give courage to the person who was grieving. We children were expected to be there as well, so all the grandchildren and great-grandchildren from nought to twenty turned up, some with snotty noses. Some sat and ate in the kitchen, some played catch in the back garden whilst my grandfather lay in the living room. There was no coffin or casket, just a dead body on a mat in the living room. We were not protected from the harshness of life. Death, we were taught, happens to all of us.

Once, while walking along in my new country, I passed a group of children with their mums; the children were looking at a dead bird. It was a pigeon, half-mauled, sides torn and bloody. One of the mums quickly pulled the children away, saying, "Oh, that bird is sleeping. Let's not disturb it." When I recounted this story to my children, they looked at me and laughed, "If that had been us, you would have said, 'Oh, that's a dead bird,' and walked off."

Moments like these made me realise that the culture of my old country sometimes clashed with my new country. There are still things that I do not feel comfortable with in the UK. I don't like the idea of elderly parents being in a nursing home or the lack of respect for older people and those in authority. In Malaysia, family ties are much more important – what happens to one member of the family impacts the whole family. In contrast, in my new country people are seen much more as individuals.

There will be times when a couple will have to compromise when they disagree over certain matters. However, being flexible and finding things that they both agree on can help to strengthen the marriage. As my friend Daisy, who moved to Australia, said, "Picking on differences is like picking on a small sore and making it worse. Rather, work at being adaptable and bringing harmony to the relationship."

We all come with our unique set of behaviours and beliefs. As someone in a cross-cultural marriage, I inhabit two cultures.

I have both my eastern ways and my newly adopted western ways. Social norms and culture do not have to divide people but can be something we can learn from each other. The unedifying qualities of one culture do not represent the whole society. We may belong to different cultural groups, but we are also individuals who are unique and different. If we really look hard, every culture has things to be celebrated and not just tolerated. We all belong to each other. Only when we start considering the 'other' as family and community can the deep wound of division heal. When we welcome strangers, we welcome God.

9

Language

"WHAT DID YOU DO WHEN YOU WENT BACK TO Malaysia?" a friend at church asked me when we got back from our summer holiday.

"We went to see the orangutans," I replied, pronouncing the word *orang-hutans*.

Just as I said the word, I immediately felt self-conscious because everyone else around me pronounced it confidently as '*ohreng yewtan*'. My pronunciation sounded out of place in my new country. Words from my culture were now owned by others. *This is confusing,* I thought. *Do I say "orang hutan" or "ohreng yewtan"?* I tend not to correct my friends' pronunciation, being unwilling to draw attention to myself.

At school, we were made to recite English words as if they were jewels in our mouths. I remember one headteacher who used to correct us, "You girls! Don't say '*tok, tok*'. You must enunciate your words properly. It's 'talk'." We were corrected on the spot and made to feel shame. English words were treated as a thing of beauty. I wonder why words taken from my culture are used without the same respect as European ones? Celebrity chefs on TV say with authority "*sembel*" instead of *sambal* and "*seytey*" instead of *sahtay*, and get away with it in a way they wouldn't if they had mispronounced the French *bain-marie.* Is there a snobbery when it comes to European words?

But what if I have given permission to allow words from my culture to be mispronounced? My French friend always makes it a point that French words are to be pronounced correctly. She offers no apology. Should I do the same? Should I sound more Malaysian or English? It was a little hard to accept being corrected about Malay words, and it took me several years to be authentic. As internationals, we have the licence to teach others the rich and colourful words of our culture. These words are to be relished in our mouths like warm-sugared beignets, savoured rather than spouted out.

Sometimes I found the meaning of English words confusing despite being able to speak the language competently. When an English friend asked, "Who did you fly with to Malaysia?" I looked at her a little confused. *Silly woman! Why does she ask me stupid questions? Who does she expect me to fly with?* So I replied, "I flew with Malcolm of course."

My friend apologised and said, "No dear, which *airline* did you use?"

"Oh, I see," I said, feeling a little stupid.

Language has historical and cultural connotations in every country. As a newcomer, it takes a while to become aware of them. Malcolm grew up familiar with grammar schools, eleven-plus, comprehensives and SATS, whilst I wondered what on earth these words meant! There was a huge gap in understanding terms like "council estate", "inner city" and "Cadbury's Cream Eggs", because I did not grow up in England. Not being familiar with these culture-specific words can be alienating. I found listening to others, observing, talking to people and asking questions helped me to grow in understanding.

One thing that shocked me as a foreign spouse was the realisation that I had to relearn the English language. Some of us may have passed our English exams at home, even getting an A*, but our new country exposes our deficiencies. At school, I was taught English by non-native speakers. My pronunciation was acceptable in Malaysia, but here in England Malcolm kept correcting me. I said "pasta" instead of "pastor" and "barry" instead of "berry", and goodness knows what I called our neighbour who was actually called Barry because by then I was so confused! I confused the children too and said "*math*" instead of "maths" and "trow" instead of "trough". An Eastern European friend who was trying to tutor her son for the eleven-plus exam said in exasperation, "My English is not good enough for me to help him for the eleven-plus. I can do the maths but not the English."

Being in a cross-cultural marriage, people assume that I know all the rules of language of my new country. I discovered language rules and taboos the hard way. Once, when I was talking to two people, I turned around to a friend and said, "She said that she's not feeling too good." The 'she' who was seated next to me exploded! "She? She? You called me she?" *Oh dear! I've clearly offended her.* I had committed a social *faux pas* even without realising it. 'She', when referring to someone, is considered rude in this country, whilst in my old country it was simply a pronoun. How easy it is to offend people without meaning to...

These are challenges someone in a cross-cultural marriage may face, but it should not allow us to lose our voice. For a long time I was uncomfortable with how I sounded, which initially stopped me from doing public things at church. I quickly learnt to be distrustful of myself when someone in church laughed at how I pronounced a word. Only when I stopped trying to prove myself did the need to be validated by others diminish.

My voice, my accent, is who I am, but sometimes I find myself becoming like a chameleon that changes colour when it senses a change in the environment or temperature. My speech changes without me realising it. Sometimes I become a native speaker, other times a foreigner, switching, shifting, swapping with ease when speaking to different people. For instance, when I talk to someone in Malaysia, I may say, "*Aiyah!* Why so hot, ah?" When I speak to someone in England, I switch to, "Oh! It's terribly hot today!"

This switching from one accent to the other is neither planned nor calculated, but is subconscious. When I am back home, I use Manglish (Malaysian English), because I want to be accepted as one of the gang. Once, when I slipped into British English, someone said accusingly, "Oh, you sound so British!" We have all met people who have lived abroad for over thirty years and have still not acquired the accent of their new country, so spending less than two years in the UK and coming home with an accent made me sound like a counterfeit! But I have learnt to accept that my inner chameleon will emerge from time to time. My family know that when I am on the phone going, "*Aiyoo!* Yes, ah? Why so bad, *lah*?" that I must be talking to someone in Malaysia.

Caught between two cultures, we sometimes forget that our old identity, language and culture are still embedded deep within us even though we may feel that we have shaken off the old country. Hannah from Slovakia speaks beautiful English, but she told me that one afternoon she overslept and her husband woke her up saying that she was late for work. She got up quickly and said, "Oh no! Oh no! I'm going to be late for work. Oh dear, what's the time?" Hannah noticed that her husband had gone strangely quiet and was staring at her. She stopped and asked him, "Why? What's wrong? Why are you staring at me?"

"Why are you speaking to me in Slovakian? I can't understand you?" he said.

They both laughed.

When working as the International Student Adviser in the UK, I was asked to help with sorting the names of students who were enrolled at twinning colleges in Malaysia for graduation. The graduation ceremony held in Kuala Lumpur was a time of great significance. Parents who had spent tens of thousands of pounds on their children's education naturally expected names to be stated correctly during the ceremony. I carefully worked through the list of student's names, knowing for example that in Chinese Malaysian families, the surname, identifying ancestral heritage, is said first. Despite my care, mistakes were made.

It is so easy to be blasé about foreign-sounding names. I know internationals who, out of consideration, have shortened their names or given themselves nicknames to make them easier to say. But would it not be a joy if we all learnt to say people's names correctly? Knowing how to say a person's name correctly shows that they matter.

Names can also show up unexpected differences between cultures. Once, as a student in California, I spotted a bunch of pre-schoolers going for a scheduled walk on campus with their teachers. A little Latino boy had his name printed large in bold letters stuck on his T-shirt. It said "Jesus". I was with my American friends and I blurted out, "His name is Jesus! Oh my goodness! His name is Jesus! How can anyone name their child Jesus!" I couldn't believe it! My American friends by now were wetting themselves with laughter. "Jesus," I found out, was pronounced differently, and in South American culture with strong Catholic ties, Jesus is a common name for a boy.

When in Malaysia, Malcolm is often addressed as Mr Malcolm instead of Mr Burrell. On a flight home, when the air stewardesses tried to figure out how to pronounce the consonants and vowels strung together in my surname, which is unfamiliar and unusual, I was embarrassed. But why, I ask myself, when Malcolm is not affected by the incorrect form of addressing him? When Malcolm is addressed as Mr Malcolm it is a sign of respect, but when my name is mispronounced it isolates me.

As internationals in cross-cultural marriages, we will no doubt pick up the lingo and colloquialisms of the language used by our partner and the new country that we are in.

When I told Malcolm, "I'm knackered!" he said, "You can't say that! Who taught you to say 'knackered'?"

"You!" I said pointing to him.

When I heard my friend, who has retained her European accent say, "Cor, blimey! It's bloomin' hot today!" I found it amusing. But it also warmed my heart. Who would have thought I would meet a European who spoke such good Cockney!

At first it was difficult to grasp the local vernacular, but it was not long before I was saying, "That bloke…" or, "That's a quid," or, "I love roasties!" Having lived in the UK now for many years, I don't have problems understanding the local jargon. Still, once in a while I discover an unexpected word, especially when colourful Uncle Frank comes to visit.

When we had a Polish live-in carer for my mother-in-law, she asked me, "What does 'It's a doddle' mean? What meaning, 'doddle'?"

I was able to say, "It means 'easy'."

"Oh, can you teach me to speak English? Maybe once a week?"

In that moment, I realised that in Stella's eyes I was British. This made me smile because it made me feel less of an outsider.

The way language is used in many cultures can sometimes be confusing because of the mannerisms and body language in that culture. Misunderstanding between my parents and Malcolm often occurred in conversations. Once, when we were driving in Malaysia and needed directions, my dad, who was sitting in the passenger seat, said to Malcolm, "Turn here."

"Where?" Malcolm asked.

"Here," my dad repeated.

By now, Malcolm was beginning to be frustrated. "But is it right or left?"

Only then did my dad say, "Turn left."

My dad used his eyes and his body leaning towards the left to indicate left, but of course, coming from another culture, Malcolm found this confusing. Malcolm needed clear, concise directions. This is cultural, whereas for a lot of Malaysians, we tend to use landmarks instead of street names and house numbers when giving directions.

Early on in our marriage, Malcolm raised his eyebrows when he heard waiters being addressed as "Boy".

For Malcolm, calling a person "boy" or "girl" was rude, whilst for most Malaysians, we have grown up with it. If the waiters were older, out of respect we would address them as "uncle" or "aunty". Waiters in restaurants are sometimes addressed as "boss". If someone wanted another beer, they would simply shout out, "Boss, one more beer!"

Malcolm found the whole way of requesting for something in a shop impolite. If we wanted the bill, we would simply say, "*Mai tan!*" ("Bill!") and if we wanted another drink, we would wave at the waiter and say, "*Satu lagi.*" ("One more.") Of course, in England, the polite way of asking would be, "Please could I have the bill?" or, "Please could I have another drink?"

Malcolm could not get his head around this. It was simply rude. But this is cultural. No one in Malaysia would consider it rude. It has taken Malcolm a while to understand this but now he is quite comfortable asking for "*Mai tan!*"

A Malaysian friend discovered that people stared at her in England when she spoke to the waiter or shop assistant without using "please" or "excuse me". Someone said to me, "Why is your friend so rude?" Yet when I first came to the UK, I was shocked that everyone called the vicar by his first name. It showed a lack of respect. In my church we addressed our vicar as "pastor". A vicar was a servant of God and not equal to us. In Malaysia respect is important.

Words can be lost in translation and do not carry the equivalent meaning in another culture, and therefore can be rude. Once when we were in Malaysia, one of the children stepped on dog poo and an elderly relative asked, "What happened? Why you step on dog shit?"

The girls found it hilarious that this elderly person swore! They squealed and laughed. I had to explain quietly that the word 'shit' did not carry the same meaning as back home. There are also words that do not cross over cultural boundaries. For example, "Holy mackerel!" in an American movie was translated to "*Sardin suci!*" in a Malaysian cinema, which literally means, "Holy sardines!"

Language can make one partner feel excluded if they are unable to understand the language used by their spouse's family and friends. Malcolm has been bored at family weddings and gatherings in Malaysia when only Tamil or Malay are spoken. When this happens, he dozes off when conversations carry on deep into the evening. Steven, whose wife is French, said, "I feel left out when we return to France. Everyone's speaking in French, including the children. I feel a little jealous."

Learning your partner's language does help. Malcolm and the children have picked up a few Tamil and Malay words, which they try to use. The moment they open their mouths to say a Malay word, everyone starts laughing at their accent and pronunciation. Malcolm does not mind being the clown. He often addresses himself as the *Mat Salleh* – the white man. Having a sense of humour is an added bonus. It has helped him to get away with making mistakes, which is often hilarious but draws people together.

Not knowing the language of a country can make the international spouse dependent on their partner. I met a young mother of two when I was volunteering at a woman's charity. She had fled domestic abuse and needed help. Unfortunately, she could hardly string together a sentence in English. The young mum missed doctor's appointments because she misunderstood the receptionist, she was afraid to go to the shops and missed postnatal groups with other mums. It was only through a health visitor who came to the house that this young mum found help. She smiled when we first met. "Where are you from?" she asked in Tamil, more curious about me than concerned about her own predicament. I realised that she was hungry for conversation, for someone she could talk to in her own language and for friendship. Then she laughed and said, "Your Tamil is very bad."

When I got to know her, I discovered that she had spent many hours on her own stuck in her flat whilst her husband was out at work. Her husband did the shopping, paid the bills and engaged with people in the outside world, whilst her inability to speak English made her a captive. It struck me that for her to gain independence and freedom, she needed to learn to speak English just as well as her husband, if not better. Domestic abuse can trap partners who do not know how to ask for help in the new country.

My aunt who came to Malaysia as a sixteen-year-old said, "I could not speak a word of Malay when I came to this country. But I made a new friend. She was a Chinese farmer who lived up the hill. Every afternoon she would come by the house and teach me Malay. I'm forever grateful to her. Learning to speak Malay gave me confidence to haggle for fish at the market, talk to the neighbours and stop depending on your uncle so much."

It is a brave thing to learn a new language, but it is also a beautiful adventure. It opens the hearts of people. When Malcolm and our daughters use their limited Malay in restaurants and shops, people respond warmly. I regret not teaching the children Malay when they were little. Poppy complained, "If only we knew Malay, we could understand all the conversations you have with the cousins. You speak so fast and it always sounds so interesting. We want to know all the juicy gossip as well."

In the UK there are various Adult Learning Colleges that offer English Language classes as well as foreign languages. Knowing the country's language helps to bridge the gaps caused by language barriers and promotes better communication within the marriage. Listening to the radio, online learning and language DVDs are other great ways to learn and listen to another language. Watching Sunday evening sitcoms when I first arrived in the UK helped me to listen to dialogues, daily conversations and small talk that defined the culture of my new country. Due to this, I acquired an ear for American English, which I found easy to listen to, whilst British English was not always so easy to grasp. Sometimes even at church I found myself unable to catch everything in the sermon because my ears had to get accustomed to an accent from a different part of the world. And then, of course, just when I thought I could understand a Brit, I discovered Welsh, Scottish, Irish, Norfolk, Geordie and other northern accents!

If you have a good grasp of the English Language but still find the vernacular difficult, take heart. It does get better over the years. The hard thing is not to feel self-conscious when words or language confuse us. We all get it wrong sometimes, but having friends who are native English speakers, joining a club, immersing in the culture and current affairs of the new country all help towards being able to use the official language of the country more confidently. Being more proficient in the language of our new country also helps us connect with others, crack a joke without insulting and gives us the independence to shine, instead of hiding in the shadow of our partner. There is something powerful about words. As a foreigner in a new land, language connects me with others and opens the door for deep and meaningful friendships. Words that speak life and hope bring people together no matter what accent we have or how badly we mispronounce a word.

10

Children

IT WAS THREE IN THE AFTERNOON AT ST JOHN'S maternity ward. Another surge of pain hit me. It was then when I heard Malcolm mumble, "I need to call my mum. She just called my mobile. Mum is worried because *your* mum is worried."

What? I could not believe it. Most women would have been given space and privacy when they are in labour, but no, not me. "Won't be long," Malcolm said, and disappeared. It turned out that mass hysteria had broken out because my parents had called our house but could not get hold of us. So the next best thing was to call Malcolm's parents.

The in-laws were blissfully unaware that we had gone to the hospital. It was a lovely summer's day. They were probably sitting outside in their immaculate garden having a nice cup of tea with a moist slice of my mother-in-law's lemon drizzle cake. Their peaceful Saturday afternoon was broken by my parents' frantic call. Panic is infectious. My normally calm in-laws awaiting the birth of their first grandchild embarked on a mission to track us down. Is this normal with other families? I suppose nothing about our family is normal!

Being in a cross-cultural marriage and being so far away from home, my parents tried to monitor the birth from afar.

We had not planned on telling them that I was in labour because I knew that being so far away, their fear would be magnified. Unfortunately, not telling them only made things worse. I discovered that things are slightly more complicated in an international marriage. We learnt not to tell every little detail to my parents. We didn't tell them that there were complications at the birth, that at one point the delivery room was packed with two consultants, three midwives, a nurse and an anxious husband. What we did say was, "You have a beautiful granddaughter." Distance makes separation hard, but distance also makes problems feel more acute. I had to navigate between disclosing enough to my parents whilst at the same time protecting them from everything.

After the drama, and the safe arrival of the baby, my mum asked, "Who does Poppy look like? Is she fair or dark?" These were the days before FaceTime. My parents waited a whole month before they received photos of their granddaughter in the post. "Oh, Poppy looks like her father," my mum said when the photos arrived. "She looks so fair." My parents, who could not see or hold Poppy, wanted as much information as possible to feel present and connected to her.

Wanting to know who the baby takes after and the colour of the baby's skin speaks about people's desire to welcome a new member to the family and celebrate family ties. Suddenly, both sides of the family longed for the baby to look like members of their own family: "She's got her dad's nose," or, "She looks just like her aunt." In some subliminal way we want to claim ownership of this new life. We all want this new little human to be part of our story.

"Who's going to look after you?" was my mum's second question. "Who's going to make you ginger and chicken soup?

Poor thing, you're all by yourself." At a time when women in my community gathered around a new mum to perform rituals and prepare nourishing foods, I was on my own. I was not cossetted by older women fussing over me, and that saddened my mum.

"Don't eat anything cold. Make sure you eat only warm foods," my mum carried on.

"Okay, Mum," I said.

"Also, don't go out in the cold. You must rest as much as possible and stay indoors."

The confinement period for most new mums in Malaysia was thirty days. This is the time when a new mum stayed indoors, kept warm and was waited on, with special food cooked for her. A new mum needed the space to pause, to regain strength and to renew her energy before she faced the monumental task of motherhood. This would have been heaven, except that I was not back home, I was in England; two days after I was discharged from the hospital, Malcolm placed the baby in the pram and announced, "It's Sunday today. Right, let's walk to church."

You must be crazy, I thought. I was sore, tired and not at all impressed, but this was England and my family was far away. I could not simply stay indoors for thirty days and expect Malcolm or his mum to wait on me. My mum was not here to watch over a pot of chicken soup simmering away for hours or prepare postpartum foods that warmed the body and helped with recovery after childbirth. Mum advised me to stay away from 'cool' food like melons, juices and cheese. But every morning, Malcolm handed me a glass of orange juice and said, "You must drink up your juice. You need your Vitamin C."

As a mum in a cross-cultural marriage, I could not always do what my old country required. It was simply not possible. Where on earth would I find traditional herbs and green leafy vegetables, and who would prepare them for me? I said thank you to Malcolm and quickly gulped down the cold, acidic orange juice even though it hurt my tummy. Even today, orange juice tastes medicinal to me.

One of the hardest things, being in a cross-cultural marriage, was not having close family nearby to help. "It's not fair, is it?" a friend once said to me. "The English mums have their mums to help out. We can't even go for an appointment without planning a two-hour exit strategy to get out of the house without a major catastrophe!"

I know this is not always true. My Welsh friend from church said, "It was hard for me too. My mum lived in Croydon and I had no help." We sometimes envy others and forget to make the best of what life gives us. Days when Poppy threw up breakfast when I was about to dart out of the door or when I had a temperature and was nursing a sore throat, self-pity crept in the door. Life as an expat mum looked so glamorous to people back home. The truth was, my hair had remnants of half-chewed baby food in it and my clothes had splodges of pureed carrots. My mother-in-law had said to me, "You don't know what this scrap of humanity is going to do to your life!"

Well, this "scrap of humanity" quite simply took over my life! The baby came to the dentist, Sainsbury's, the changing room and even insisted on accompanying me to the toilet! I could not bring myself to call up Malcolm's mum, who lived thirty miles away, and ask, "Oh, by the way, I need to get the shopping. Could you come over and help, please?"

Once when I was still learning the ropes as a new mum, whilst out shopping, I left the baby behind, still strapped in the trolley, and returned to the car. It was only when I was about to get into the driver's seat that I realised I had forgotten my small human. Heart thumping madly, I ran back to the trolley park to find my daughter sitting contentedly, totally unaware of any crisis.

I missed the support of my own family. But when my mum called and asked, "How are you doing? Are you able to cope by yourself?" I was even more determined not to fail. As a friend said, "You just get on with it. There is no one to help, but you just simply learn to be resilient. You learn to be independent because everyone else has their own lives." The danger for all new mums, and maybe especially those whose families are far away, is that we feel like we need to be superwomen. However, one thing I have learnt is that we shouldn't be afraid to ask for help. One of the most courageous things any new mum could say is, "Help, I can't do this on my own."

Some mums we knew turned up with hand-me-down baby equipment and clothes, which I was grateful for. These women were helpful without being pushy, and supported me during those crucial first weeks of coping as a new mum. Attending the parents and toddlers' group at church helped me meet other mums. This became a secure place where I could ask questions about teething, potty training and schooling. I am still in touch with Daphne who ran this group for all of us new mums. There's something comforting about meeting other mums who have children the same age as yours. Also, finding groups that will support you gets you out of the house. The children will get used to seeing other people as well. God sent heroes in my life in the shape of women in my church who helped look after the girls when I was ill. The shape of the traditional family looks different for us, but it does not mean that there are not people who will help if we need it. There is much kindness in the hearts of the people of this country.

Raising a child in a cross-cultural marriage meant that one set of grandparents missed out. I felt a tinge of guilt that I had robbed my parents of the joy of watching my children grow up. We tried to make amends with annual visits home, but there remained a huge hole in my parents' life. They missed Poppy and Willow dearly. Once, after we had returned home from a two-week holiday in my parents' home, my dad said, "The house is deadly silent now. But when I close my eyes, I can still hear their laughter and see their faces."

The reality is, being a far-away grandparent is tough. Telephone calls and birthday cards from Poppy and Willow have brought a lot of joy to my parents, but they are not the same as being there in person together. Nowadays, with FaceTime and WhatsApp, calling up family and singing happy birthday has made such a difference. However, for Poppy and Willow, this is what they have always known. They have learnt to compartmentalise, and their Malaysian grandparents are associated with summer holidays. They do not seem particularly affected by growing up with only one set of grandparents.

Just once, Poppy remarked, "We don't have a lot of relatives here like other people in my class." This happened during festive holidays when everyone else seemed busy with their own extended families. Malcolm's family was small, and not belonging to a large extended family made the girls feel that they missed out. The grass is always greener... British friends have complained about the difficulties of extended families and expenses at Christmas times. There is no perfect family. When Poppy and Willow envy their friends who have had one generation after another attend the same school, have always lived in the same street and have cousins and aunties nearby, I simply say, "Look at what an international family you belong to! You have cousins in Malaysia, Australia and New Zealand. Imagine going around the world and having people you can visit."

Differences in culture can sometimes be seen in the expectations that others in the family have – even over small matters such as the name of a new baby. When Suzanna and Praveen had their child, they decided to call her Cecilia. "What type of name is that?" Praveen's mum asked over the phone. "Why can't you give her a nice Indian name?" Suzanna and Praveen both live in Australia. Suzanna is Chinese and Praveen is Indian and they both decided that giving their daughter a western name would help her to blend in better in their newly adopted country. But Praveen's mum, living thousands of miles away in Malaysia, wanted an Indian name. Giving the baby an Indian name would somehow provide a little compensation for the fact that Praveen had married a Chinese lady and not someone of a similar race.

A few months after our daughter was born, my mother-in-law had taken to enquiring after the baby's sleeping habits. "Is our baby sleeping through the night yet?" As if to make me look like a bad mother, Poppy refused to play ball and woke up every two hours, not sleeping throughout the night until she was three. "Oh, Malcolm slept through the night when he was just three months old," his mother reminded me.

Nice for you, I thought. *Does my mother-in-law think I have a magic wand to simply wave over Poppy to get her to sleep through the night?* I found this question stressful, added on top of all the various emotions battling inside me as a new mum. Coming from Malaysia, we worry less about sleep and bedtimes as the hot sticky nights mean that children go to bed later. But I was worn out most evenings, so even though early bedtimes in England surprised me, I gave in to the luxury of having a quiet evening. I liked the order and structure of having a proper bedtime as opposed to falling asleep naturally. Is there one correct way? Looking back now, I wish I had been more relaxed about all this, but a cross-cultural relationship meant sometimes having to make an intentional choice about following the accepted norms of my newly adopted country. If you are a parent from another culture, have the courage to go with gut instincts about bedtimes and parenting, but most of all, enjoy every stage your child is at without feeling guilty.

The first time we were invited out for dinner, Malcolm suggested getting a babysitter. When our babysitter arrived, I eyed her suspiciously. What kind of society is this that trusts a sixteen-year-old with a baby? When we were little, we were not left behind. We were taken to weddings, meals and family gatherings. Of course, I remember many an evening as a young child trying hard to stay awake as the women gossiped away into the night. In Malaysia children are not hidden away once it is dark but are included in most family gatherings. I did not always like the strict, regimented bedtimes that parenting books in England advised new parents. But as the partner who was the foreigner, I knew I had to adjust to new ways, including a new perspective on parenting.

Despite cultural differences, most couples I talked to shared common goals when it came to how to raise their children. Rachel is a Malaysian married to an American. She said, "Even though we grew up in different parts of the world, we discovered that our values are the same, we watched the same TV programmes and we came from similar backgrounds. When it came to raising our daughter, there weren't any issues."

Perhaps in some subconscious way we are attracted to a person who shares the same values as us. This makes parenting a lot easier. Malcolm and I discovered that when it came to how to raise Poppy and Willow, our values and beliefs were the same. We share the same faith, and our attitude towards money, punctuality and work is similar too.

When it came to raising our children, our biblical values have had a big impact on our children. These values are neither British nor Malaysian, but values that teach them that they are loved by God, that their lives have a purpose and that they have been uniquely and wonderfully created. We found that godly values transcend cultural values. They have given clarity to our children as they navigate their way through a world that sometimes sends mixed messages.

Food has always been central in my culture. When I started weaning the children, I introduced sauces with ginger, garlic and onion. Malcolm's mum observed me quietly and then, when she could no longer hold it in, expressed her concerns: "Why, we can't have our baby smelling of garlic when she starts school!"

Smelling of garlic had been the last thing on my mind. I stopped feeding the children garlic when my mother-in-law visited but snuck it in behind her back.

Having other people's children over on play dates was a real eye-opener. I discovered a new category of food altogether. A few of Poppy and Willow's friends did not eat "green things" on their plates. To ensure that Poppy and Willow still had friends at school, I started filling our freezer with smiley faces, potato waffles and chicken nuggets. The girls were delighted. "Yay!" they cheered. "Whenever we have friends over, we get to eat smiley faces!"

But having friends over from school revealed cultural differences in ways that I least expected. There were times when I wished I had not opened my mouth. Coming from a culture that does not make a huge fuss of Santa, Malcolm and I discussed candidly with the children about the existence of Father Christmas. We didn't have any problems with this until one day when Poppy's classmate Charlie came to visit on a play date. Charlie was seven and was in the same class as Poppy. After dinner was served, I left Charlie and Poppy with their tea and went to the next room. But then I heard arguing and rushed back into the kitchen. Just as I walked in, I heard Charlie say, "But Santa *is* real!"

"Santa does not exist. He's not real!" Poppy corrected him.

It was almost Christmas. Charlie was waiting for his presents from Santa, and now a girl had said that Santa was a fake. I could have died. I had no idea how to get out of this mess.

"Santa is real! He's real!" cried Charlie.

"No, he's not. You can ask my mum," Poppy said looking defiantly and victoriously at me.

Poor Charlie burst into tears and said, "I'm going to tell my mum! You're all lying."

I knew that I would not be forgiven. The next morning in the school playground, I approached Carlie's mum gingerly. She did not look happy. I apologised profusely, but I'm pretty sure I was now thoroughly in her bad books. Poppy was never invited back to Charlie's house. At that point, I felt like a true immigrant with little understanding of my new country.

Fitting in at the school playground becomes a focal point for all of us as parents when our children are in primary school. I have had to remind myself that children are only at primary school for a short time. We should be proud of who we are as a parent from another culture. We don't need to always conform but can have the confidence to celebrate who we are. It is also important to have a life outside of the school playground.

It was a relief that despite my close encounters with British mothers in the school playground, Poppy and Willow were well-liked by their classmates. The truth is, children are often more gracious and forgiving than adults.

For us parents from another culture and unaccustomed to the traditions of the new country, the growing-up years are a learning experience. When I lost a milk tooth as a child, Grandmother would say, "Quick, give me your tooth. We must not show it to the sky or it will not grow back." She would then clutch it in her fist as we children followed her out to the garden where she would dig and bury my milk tooth deep inside the darkness of the soil. In my new country I had to learn about the Tooth Fairy. I had to learn that parents had to replace the tooth with a 50p coin, or whatever the going rate was, which seemed to depend on which parent you talked to in the school playground. And after the 'Charlie' incident, Poppy insisted that we left mince pies out for Santa by the fireplace.

Raising children is a privilege and not a burden. But there was a constant tension, where I tried to find a balance between my old and new country. Young people in the UK crave independence and grow up fast, whilst it is the opposite in my old country. I'm not sure which way is right, but I have met wonderful parents from both cultures who anchor the family, keep their children safe and show them that they are loved.

Identity can be an issue for some children from cross-cultural relationships. Children born to parents from different cultures will undoubtedly be different. The differences could be little things like having a preference for certain types of food. As Malcolm says, "When it comes to food, your Malaysian side wins!"

I asked Nadine, who is half French and half English, "Do you identify yourself as French or British?"

"Definitely British," she said, "but my stomach is French."

Poppy and Willow definitely prefer Malaysian food. Coming from two cultures they have an innate curiosity about food from other cultures and find it boring simply eating food from one continent. Other times, identity can mean behaving differently depending on where they are. When in Malaysia, Poppy and Willow remember to address relatives who are older than them as "Aunty" or "Uncle" but slip back to first names when we return to England. Poppy and Willow sound British, and when they try to speak Malay, they have a foreign accent. They will always stand out as the 'foreign' cousins due to the way they speak. Their mannerisms and taste in fashion are English and they identify themselves as British. Identity is not something they have had to struggle with. When people ask them, "Where are you from?" they love telling people of their mixed heritage. For others, being of mixed nationality means belonging always to two countries. There is a sense of not belonging totally to either but being a part of both, which can create a sense of feeling displaced.

For others, Brexit has changed how they want to identify themselves. My friend Joanna, originally from Ireland but now living in England, said, "Brexit changed things for my girls." Joanna's daughters, who are in their twenties, saw Brexit as something deeply personal. To split from the EU felt like a separation from Ireland. They wanted to identify themselves as Irish, to reclaim their heritage as a retaliation for the split. After Brexit, they immediately went and applied for an Irish passport.

Children from cross-cultural marriages are enriched from having a rich heritage of belonging to two cultures. Poppy and Willow learnt about the differences in our culture, history and tradition not from books but from growing up in an international family. Some children may face challenges arising from the fact that how they look seemingly contradicts who they are. But when people ask Poppy and Willow, "Where are you from? Spain? Are you Arabic?" being of mixed-parentage is a compliment. They like being different because it makes them feel unique.

Sometimes children from cross-cultural marriages may find belonging hard. While their parents belong to one distinct culture, the children are a fusion of both. But even hard things, with support and understanding, can help children from cross-cultural marriages find their own voice and place in society. The fact that they are of mixed race is a blessing. In a world that is fast becoming diverse, belonging to two cultures can be empowering. We need the voices of people who defy stereotypes and race. God loves us exactly how we are. He celebrates every child as beautiful, breathtaking and a masterpiece.

11

The Pandemic

IT WAS 18TH MARCH 2020. I CLICKED ON THE Malaysian online news. The breaking story about the full lockdown was followed by a picture of the army at the Malaysia-Singapore border where roadblocks had shut the entry point between the two countries. This was unprecedented. Stakes were high and I was totally unprepared.

Covid-19 was unexpected. The pandemic revealed the fragility of all our lives. It exposed our vulnerability and our reliance on the certainty of air travel that kept us connected and linked to our families. It jolted me from my secure world where borders were crossed and oceans were flown over in less than twenty-four hours. The pandemic made me look at distance differently. I had been lulled into believing that my mum was only fourteen hours away from me. But the fourteen-hour flight back home was not going to happen this year.

The worst thing for those of us who are spouses in a cross-cultural marriage is that we are stuck. Business travellers could return home, holidaymakers were made sure of a swift return, and students in their gap year managed to book the last flight back. But for those of us who are foreign spouses, our native country was beyond our reach.

I felt like a ladybird on its back with its legs dangling in the air. No matter how hard I tried, I was in the same position, legs frantically moving, kicking the air, frustration mounting and desperation overwhelming me. This was all a bad dream, I tried to convince myself. Then it struck me that there was absolutely nothing that I could do. "Don't worry," Malcolm had said. "It'll all calm down by the summer. I'm sure we can see your mum in August."

Malcolm's optimism gave me hope for a short while. Then the news came. Malaysia announced that all UK nationals were banned from entering the country because of the soaring infections in the UK. There was not going to be a trip home in the foreseeable future. Why did I feel so bad, I wondered. If Mum had been younger and had other family members with her, would I feel the same? The fact that Mum was by this point all by herself following Dad's death in 2013 made things worse. Time was running out. An invisible weight sat heavily on me. I stayed close to any news I could get, but as the days rolled into weeks, and the weeks into months, the hidden roots of my life that sprawled beneath oceans and boundaries and connected me to my old home began to wither.

Then anger crept inside me like an uninvited guest. I welcomed it. Every jogger on the footpath who came too close to me, every shopper who leaned into me, every person who broke lockdown rules and did not keep to social distancing became the enemy keeping me away from my mum. When we are desperate, we blame others. Ongoing travel restrictions made me feel trapped.

A friend Rose, who is French, had not seen her mum for over a year. She told me about how her neighbour had complained about the lockdown saying, "I haven't seen my mum for eight months." Rose replied, "I too have not seen my mum. You know now how I feel when every day is a day without my mum." Rose expected sympathy, perhaps even understanding. Her neighbour looked at her and said, "It's different for you. It's your choice that you are here. It's not my choice that I can't see my mum."

For us internationals, our elderly parents and families are invisible to those around us, our connections with them considered of even less importance, perhaps because, after all, we *did* choose this expat life. It made me feel more reluctant to talk about how the separation imposed by the pandemic affected me. Other people's problems seemed more urgent and immediate than a foreigner's elderly parent thousands of miles away. Yet for Rose, whose father is ninety, and for me, whose mum is eighty-six, the prospect of our elderly parents dying is real and potentially imminent. Every day that passed became a day of maybes and what-ifs. I did not want others to offer solutions. I simply wanted someone to listen. Just because we have chosen a cross-cultural marriage does not mean that the pain of separation is somehow less.

Before Covid, every year my dear mum would ask, "When are you coming home?" Mum clings to our annual visit as if it is her lifeline, the buoy that keeps her afloat since Dad died. Covid-19 kept us nailed to one location. When front pages of newspapers flashed with images of elderly being hugged by their families, I wished my mum was with me. Home never felt more distant and God seemed silent.

Lockdown has been a time of soul-searching for me. My annual flights home had made me presumptuous. It was a given that each year I would have the luxury of flying home, hiring a car, seeing my mum, visiting friends, erasing the guilt that I carried the rest of the time. My once-a-year visit had made me believe that I was doing all that I could for my mum. However, the pandemic has made me rethink her care.

The truth is that those of us who are in a cross-cultural marriage find ourselves holding two roles. We are a parent and a spouse in the UK as well as a child to someone else in a faraway country. Our ears have grown accustomed to hearing the sound of two different drumbeats in our lives. I felt pulled by my sense of responsibility as a parent but also by my guilt as a daughter who needed to be there for her mum in her old age. All kinds of emotions that I did not think existed bubbled to the surface. Morbid questions tormented me at night as I tossed and turned. What if Mum gets Covid? Who will sort out the funeral arrangements? Sleep evaded me. I was so conscious of the time when my father became ill in 2013 – I missed the flight home due to a fatality on the M25. Three hours later when I arrived at Heathrow, the Malaysian Airlines plane had left without me. By the time I caught the next flight, I was too late; my dad was in a coma and died the following morning.

For many, the separation has been painful. "I haven't seen my sisters for four years," said one lady called Nina, who was not able to make annual visits during the pandemic. There are others like me where whole families have emigrated, leaving elderly parents to fend for themselves. Pre-Covid, our elderly parents were able to shop and look after themselves. The pandemic stripped them of their independence and isolated them from their communities.

A friend in church who thought he was being helpful said, "Has your mum not got any cousins nearby?" But cousins, no matter how caring, are not a solution for the elderly with all their children overseas. The penalty for travelling out of state was high, and I could not expect my aunts and cousins to put themselves in a vulnerable position. The fact is, having a parent abroad is complicated, care is messy and there is always a sense of carrying an invisible burden. The sparkle and glamour of expat life was replaced by the dullness and monotony of living in lockdown thousands of miles away from home. When we face uncertainty, we want the connection with family. As an international living in the UK, I became obsessed with news from home. I needed to know everything that was happening in my old country. I needed to rescue Mum.

The pandemic gave me a new language – the language of lament. Lament became my cry to God. Psalm 77:1 says, "I cried out to God for help; I cried out to God to hear me." I cried in silence, I cried with words and sometimes I was simply numb. "You all don't know how I feel," I said to Malcolm. "It's so easy for you. Everything and everyone you want is here. Me, I can't even help my mum." I no longer knew how to fix things. So much of my time was invested in taming my future because the present had spiralled out of control. Could I in some way control the future? Could I fast-forward from the present? But as I cried out to God, my focus shifted from my present circumstances to Him. I realised that my present in which I had no control was just as important to Him as my future. God is a God who is nearby, not distant and separate from my present, which I wanted to get rid of.

The present which was unpredictable and hostile became the very thing that helped me. Lament reminded me of the faithfulness of God even when I had absolutely no idea how long this chaos would last. God is attentive to our cries. When I sat and watched in dismay that British Airways had stopped all flights to Kuala Lumpur, God reminded me of hope. I had focused so much on what I *could not* do that I lost clarity of what I *could* do. I could still help from afar. True, I could not see my mum, but I could still connect with her. I could still send her gifts and reminders that she was not forgotten. There was a glimmer of hope instead of crushing despair. Only God can fix things.

Oh, the wonders of international online shopping! To find I could sit in our home in England and buy groceries from Tesco in Kuala Lumpur was a breakthrough. When an elderly friend in church asked me, "So what are you doing today?" I said, "Buying vegetables online from Tesco to be sent to my mum!"

My friend paused. Then he looked at me a little puzzled. "You mean the Tesco van manages to get to Kuala Lumpur in time?" He had visions of the Tesco delivery van leaving our local store and driving all the way to Kuala Lumpur! We laughed!

Stuck at home in lockdown, Mum started getting her weekly groceries. She had something to look forward to every week. Each week she would ask, "So, when is the Tesco van coming?" It was a relief for me to ask over a video call, "What would you like to eat next week? Would you like another bar of Cadbury's chocolate?" Special treats like pizza, fries, chocolates, ice-cream and cakes turned up at her front door! I no longer felt helpless. I was in control of something. My mum was no longer scared that she would run out of food. The sight of the delivery van arriving outside her house every Monday morning was like Christmas for Mum. It was a small gesture but made such a difference for both of us. Most of all, it made my mum feel secure, and that gave me peace of mind. Of course, it is not smooth-going all the time. Even at this point of writing, as lockdown has been extended in Malaysia, food delivery has been unpredictable. I am learning not to get distressed, but to find instead new ways of getting food to Mum. And there is still so much to celebrate and give thanks to God for. I managed to download the app and got an appointment for my mum for her Pfizer vaccination. Her carer said that although most of the elderly at the vaccination centre were with family members, the nurses and doctors were especially kind to my mum. Incidents like these assured me of God's unwavering grace.

For others, the cost of the pandemic has been harder. For those in the UK, the pandemic has made some come face to face with anti-foreign sentiments. A friend who has European and Chinese ancestry said she felt uncomfortable travelling on the Tube in London. The other commuters stared at her and sat away from her. Has the pandemic split us further based on the colour of our skin, our racial features and how we speak?

For those living in other countries, different issues have made the pandemic especially hard. Filipino friend Christy, who lives in the Far East, talked about women in relationships with other internationals who have lost their daily wage and income. There are food banks in some countries, but a foreigner in a new country still has very few rights. Christy said her friends, mainly domestic workers, have grouped together and supported each other with whatever money they have. Unfortunately, their suffering is twofold. For a lot of them, whatever money they had been earning before the pandemic was also sent home to support their families struggling to make ends meet in the Philippines.

Tina is also from the Philippines but is married to an Englishman and lives in England. Three years ago, Tina and her family moved from the Philippines to the UK because of their sons' education. Moving to a new village, Tina simply could not slot into the lives of the other English mums as her English was not very good. Tina tracked down other Filipino care workers and nurses near her village through WhatsApp and Facebook. This has been her lifeline. However, lockdown slammed the brakes on any social gatherings with people from home. For Tina, these meetings were her strong cup of cocoa and warm blanket. This was where she felt understood without having to try. Tina misses the group but has found solace in keeping in touch through social media. Yet she still talks about going home. "That's where we would like to settle down for good when the boys have grown up," she said. The pandemic has convinced her that the new country could never be home.

Having a local Asian grocery store nearby has helped her keep the reminders from home fresh and present. Food has been such a solace for so many of us. Never before have I searched the internet on how to cook street food from Malaysia. Eating food from home is about remembering, and for me this has been especially important as I am unable to make a visit any time soon.

In the past we tried to find the perfect time to visit family abroad, because our lives were so busy. The pandemic has taught me about what really matters. It also helped me understand a little about the real pain of those in true exile from their beloved country. I have become more grateful. And this has affected my children too. There is a new clarity about the importance of their annual pilgrimage to their second home in Malaysia, so familiar yet foreign. "We had taken our visits to see *Pati* for granted. We never knew how fortunate we were," Willow said. "Oh, the days when we could simply hop on a plane to see her!"

My daughters long not just for their grandma but for a country that knows their name. Perhaps they too inhabit two worlds and will always do so despite having their feet firmly planted in one.

My phone buzzed non-stop those early days of the pandemic. Being an international meant belonging to group chats with other Malaysians scattered all over the globe. Friends started texting, "What's happening to the UK? Has the situation in the UK gone downhill?"

There was news flying around on social media. According to a senior politician in Singapore, Covid-19 had created "a pandemic of misinformation". The world saw the pandemic from different eyes. As someone inhabiting two worlds, I began to see two versions of the same narrative. When I sent a friend overseas the link to the BBC's report on the source of the pandemic, my information was dismissed. "Shame on the BBC for reporting false news," she said.

My friends from home were listening to a new rhetoric. Misinformation spread like wildfire. It rewrote the story of the world's suffering as 'us' and 'them'. Has it made us more tribal? I felt caught between two worlds. It hit me that as someone in a cross-cultural marriage, my perspective compared to someone from my old country looked vastly different. I held in my hands two opposing views because I belonged to two places. At times it was difficult to distinguish fake news from truth. And at other times I chose to be silent because my views would appear so confrontational. Perhaps, as someone who inhabits two worlds, I can be a moderator of truth. Being in a cross-cultural marriage forces me to weigh up different opinions and views on the pandemic. I see events differently because my heart is not tethered only to one place. At a time when the world is suspicious and bewildered, there is an opportunity to offer another perspective. Truth has become more fluid, but as a person who belongs to two cultures, the language required of me is honesty, empathy and compassion.

As I write this, it has been two years since I last saw my dear mum. Hope keeps me grounded: that things will get better; that we will be able to step foot in the country left behind and kiss our loved ones again. There are good days and there are difficult days, but Malcolm and I feel that we must look forward. We have started planning for our next trip to Malaysia despite our flights being cancelled three times already. Whilst every string of our connection seems to have been axed, we are convinced that it is important to plan our next trip. So we have booked our next flight. Now we wait. Psalm 27:14 says, "Wait for the LORD; be strong and take heart and wait for the LORD." Something is daring about hope. It is looking at situations beyond our control and handing them to God. It is saying, "I trust You, Lord. You've got this."

12

Belonging

"GOOD EVENING, LADIES AND GENTLEMEN. THIS IS your captain speaking. Welcome to flight BA34 to Heathrow. The weather in London tomorrow is forecast to be sunny and clear with highs of twenty-two degrees."

It was 3rd August 2019, months before anyone had heard of Covid-19. The deep, rich English voice, both familiar and known, warmed my soul. For two weeks we had been seeing family and friends in Kuala Lumpur. I hadn't missed England. But aboard the British Airways flight, the English captain's voice brought back memories of my other 'home'. The wonderful British accent was like an old friend I had not seen for a while! I could not tell you the precise moment when I stopped looking at England as a foreign land. It happened subtly over time. Yet still today, when I am in England and take a flight returning to Malaysia, I am excited. The faces of people, brown-skinned and sunburnt, are the faces I realise that I have missed. Home has become a place that I can no longer contain in a single box. It has become split between two places that I both belong to and that belong to me.

In a sense I am a nomad who returns to familiar trails. But I also know that my one true connection to Malaysia is my mum. Perhaps I will stop yearning to return home when she is no longer alive. Separated by oceans and mountains, I keep exploring new ways to be a better daughter, how to care for her and how to sustain a long-distance relationship with her.

For now, my place in my old home has changed. The gaps in my relationships with some friends and relatives are noticeable but unspoken. I am no longer a true Malaysian. WhatsApp group messages with old university friends talk about a life that is separate to mine. I have become a distant friend, and a stranger to the real struggles of Malaysians. I have become a mere onlooker. Birthdays, engagements, weddings and baptisms take place without me. Some of the foreign spouses I talked to said that the thing they missed most was not celebrating these special occasions with parents and siblings. For me, it was not the celebrations but the deaths. This was harder than missing birthdays.

When I first visited home after a year of being in the UK, friends and family were warm and friendly, but I could not simply slot back into their lives. My cousin had had a baby, a friend had got married, a single friend had become an aunt, and generally people were busy with their own lives. I had moved out of their lives and had to relearn how to establish old relationships. For those of us in cross-cultural marriages abroad, I have found that the onus depends on us to maintain a relationship. People are busy, so if I valued their relationship, I had to stay connected with family and friends, keep in touch and visit them. Over the years, this has become easier as we made more regular visits home, and praying with others over Zoom and video calls has strengthened ties.

On the other hand, I have a place in my new country, in my new community, and I have people who belong to me. When I returned to England after a two-week holiday in Malaysia, my widowed English neighbour said, "It's so comforting to have you back."

And so here I am, a wife, mother, sister and friend from a faraway land, because my heart has been tugged and pulled to a foreign place. Some have called people like me "brave", others have shaken their heads and muttered, "Fool!" Being in a cross-cultural marriage and having to move abroad is a bit like mountain-climbing. There are times when the trail becomes difficult to navigate, where the only way up is to go on all fours.

Coming to a new country forced me to learn new things outside my comfort zone. At other times, the experience was simply mesmerising when the sun pierced through the clouds on the mountaintop and lit up the dark corners of the valleys. I have enjoyed meeting new people and exploring my new country – a country which continues to surprise me. But mountaintop experiences can be short-lived, a fleeting moment until the sun disappears and heavy mist descends. For me as an international spouse, the sudden death of loved ones threw me into disarray. I could not return home long enough to stay with my mum when Dad died. Mum needed someone to pick up the pieces, but I had to rush home for an eleven-year-old starting senior school. There were hard choices that had to be made. Each day demanded trust in a God who knows me more than I know myself.

A bit like mountain-climbing, my experiences allowed me to discover beauty along the way, as well as what I was capable of. How many adventures do we miss when we give in to doubts? When I asked two of my good friends if they regretted making that choice to marry a foreigner, they said no. Has life been hard for them? Yes, but all marriages have their challenges.

Looking back at the past twenty-five years of being in the UK, life has been a series of adventures, of exploring a new country, of discovering new friends and finding freedom to be myself. The challenges in a cross-cultural relationship do not need to break a couple but instead can help each one to move towards beauty and towards deeper love.

There are days when the heartbeat of my new country is louder than that of my old country. Nonetheless, if in my new country I simply watch from the sidelines, I am effectively rejecting my place here. As spouses in cross-cultural marriages, we may not always feel qualified to contribute to our new community. To shut ourselves away because we feel inadequate is to rob ourselves and others.

Sadly, I have met people who say, "I'll never feel at home here." But I have found that only by embracing my new country and people did I start feeling less of an outsider. Setting up a homework club for primary school children brought me face to face with foreign mums who, like me, were trying to find their way in a new country. I met mums from Poland, Romania, Bulgaria, France and India. I would not have had the opportunity to connect with so many women from different parts of the world had I not been here in England. For this I am richer.

We have all made our choices. God does not make mistakes and He is bigger than our decisions. Sometimes it requires us to step out and embrace the new life before us. When I first came to the UK as a foreign wife, I struggled with feeling relevant. My experience depended on whether I was accepted or rejected. I had no history in this new place. I had to start afresh when it came to every relationship, my career and even knowing who I was. But I also came face to face with something new – that people around me were deep down just the same as me. Every one of us yearns for belonging.

There are many things about this country that endear themselves to me. I like how every team is celebrated in sports, even those that do not quite make it. I admire the opportunities given to those with disabilities when so many places in the world disregard them. On the first day of term when Chen, an exchange teacher from another country, stood outside a special needs school to welcome the new students, she wept uncontrollably. "In my country, we hide the disabled," she said.

I see white men with black women and my heart is full, because in my culture dark-skinned women are considered not beautiful. I admire the way foreigners are welcomed here. Yes, the people will not always get it right, but the UK as a nation is tolerant. Sunita, who is from Trinidad, said, "When I first came to England to study nursing, I missed home. In class one day, a lecturer handed us a bowl that contained names of people from a church nearby. She said we could pick a name with a telephone number attached to it. That person would be a friend whilst we were in England." Sunita said that she picked Mrs Young's name. "Mrs Young took me to Sainsburys. She explained what a penny was and helped me. Mrs Young has since died but I still keep in touch with her son." This was forty years ago but Sunita remembers this event as life-defining. Someone had taken an interest in her. Thirty years after meeting her, Sunita came back to church because of what Mrs Young had done.

About twenty-five years ago, when I came to this country, I was a stranger. Now my name is inscribed in the hearts of people who call me friend. I am humbled. Recently I received a text from Claire, who is English: "I wanted to thank you for being such a good friend to me and making me laugh." Claire has been a wonderful friend to me. In all our years as mums trying to sort out our children, we never saw ourselves as 'other' but simply as two mums who have tried to do our best for our children. Many others like Claire made room in their hearts for me, and I thank God for them. It is through people like Claire that God showed me that cultural values and norms which are totally different to mine can be understood rather than simply tolerated. There will always be things that I do not like about my new country, but no country is perfect. I no longer look for perfection but for what connects me to another person.

I am grateful to God for bringing Malcolm and me together. Growing up, when I had imagined what my future would look like, it certainly didn't include the UK. But I feel blessed to be here and married to Malcolm, who has always treated me as his equal. He respects me and allows me to be the person I am. We have been on this journey together. Whilst I have had to adjust to a new culture, Malcolm has also taken an interest in my culture, language and food. It has not been one-sided.

When we now return to Kuala Lumpur, I drink in the familiar sights of my old country. There are new roads, new buildings and quite a lot of foreigners. After picking up the hire car, we drive to my mum's place. Approaching the road that leads to her house, everything feels familiar and known. There are rows of stalls with vendors selling fruits, noodles and deep-fried jackfruit and bananas. I can almost savour the sweet, sticky taste of hot jackfruit melting in my mouth. Everything looks colourful and bright, even the blood red rambutans and pink guava piled high at the stalls. The noise of the motorbikes honking as they zigzag between cars and the squealing of a family of monkeys on telephone wires remind me that I am home. I welcome the sights and sound as if meeting an old friend again. I notice little things about my old country, the things I had taken for granted, the open smiles of the people, their gentleness and warmth of spirit. Yet I know something has changed. The place looks the same, the smells are the same, the people look familiar, but I have changed and the country has grown up without me.

I see the world through a different lens because I have been carved by two different cultures. Like two mighty rivers that have cut through my life, creating new paths, flattening rough terrains, changing the landscape and merging, I am a product of two countries and will always be so. I understand myself better – knowing deep within me that I could never now be nailed to one place. There will always be a restlessness in my spirit. But that is okay, because I am only a sojourner on this planet for a moment. My true home is in Christ. It is okay not to feel rooted. For now, I will count my blessings and choose contentment, living fully in the country I find myself in.

Acknowledgements

I would like to thank God for giving me the opportunity to write this book and for leading me to the right people who enabled me to put this story together. Without God this would not have been possible. I am also grateful for the support and encouragement of my husband Malcolm and my two daughters.

I would like to thank Marion Angold, Annie and Malcolm Kidd, Pam Stunt and Alan Webb for reading through some of my chapters and for their kind words; and Fiona Linday, my mentor who read my book, made corrections and who inspired me to finish what I had started – thank you.

I would also like to thank Vim and Pat, who prayed with me and encouraged me. Finally, a huge thanks to all who gave up their time to complete the questionnaire and share a bit of their own journey. You have taught me so much.

Sheela Burrell

About the Author

Sheela Burrell studied Creative Writing at California State University, Fresno where she was given the Distinguished Graduate Student award for 1992 from The Department of English in the School of Humanities. Whilst in the US, Sheela had her first short story, *The Flood*, published in *Common Wages*, the university journal. Upon obtaining her MA in Creative Writing, Sheela returned home to her job as an English teacher in a secondary school in Malaysia and later worked as a lecturer at a higher education college in Kuala Lumpur.

Sheela is married to Malcolm, whom she met whilst he was working in Malaysia, and they now live in Essex with their two daughters. After coming to live in the UK in 1996, Sheela worked with young adults at a further education college and later with international students at a local university. She enjoys teaching and in 2016 started a homework club for primary school children. At her church, she works with children and teenagers.